Cost Shifting in Health Care

Cost Shifting in Health Care

Separating Evidence from Rhetoric

Michael A. Morrisey

The AEI Press

Publisher for the American Enterprise Institute
WASHINGTON, D.C.

1994

Distributed to the Trade by National Book Network, 15200 NBN Way, Blue Ridge Summit, PA 17214. To order call toll free 1-800-462-6420 or 1-717-794-3800. For all other inquiries please contact the AEI Press, 1150 Seventeenth Street, N.W., Washington, D.C. 20036 or call 1-800-862-5801.

Library of Congress Cataloging-in-Publication Data

Morrisey, Michael A.
    Cost shifting in health care : separating evidence from rhetoric / Michael A. Morrisey.
       p.   cm.
    Includes bibliographical references.
    ISBN 0-8447-3860-3. — ISBN 0-8447-3861-1 (pbk.)
    1. Medical care, Cost of—United States.   2. Medical care—Cost shifting—United States.   I. Title.
RA410.5.M67   1994
338.4'33621'0973—dc20   94-14605
                                                   CIP

ISBN 0-8447-3860-3 (cloth)
ISBN 978-0-8447-3861-1

The AEI Press
Publisher for the American Enterprise Institute
1150 17th Street, N.W., Washington, D.C. 20036

To Michelle and David,
who enjoy going to the movies

Acknowledgments

Thanks are due to Mahmud Hassan, who participated in long debates as this monograph progressed; to Bryan Dowd, Bob Helms, and Joyce Lanning, who made extensive comments on earlier drafts; and to Cheryl Weissman, who carefully polished an otherwise clumsy effort. Remaining errors are my own.

Contents

1

Cost Shifting Is Everywhere—Or So It Seems

I left work early last week and took my kids to the movies. The price of admission to the 5:00 P.M. showing is only $3.00; the adult admission is $7.00 both earlier in the afternoon and later in the evening. Having read too many stories of cost shifting in health care markets, I thought it too bad that the theater operator was able to charge 5:00 P.M. moviegoers only $3.00. Does this mean that she has had to raise the price of tickets to the more affluent early and late moviegoers to cover her costs?

Since the movie wasn't very good, I started wondering about ticket pricing strategies. I imagined a discussion with the theater owner in which I asked her why the evening showings were so expensive. She said that the film distributors kept raising their fees and that the mall was always raising the rent on the space. She also said that pricing the 5:00 P.M. showing was a serious problem. "We would like to charge more at that time," she said, "and have even tried to do so. But those people just wouldn't pay more. So, we have to charge the other patrons more."[1]

This led me to ponder the public policy prescriptions that could be advanced to solve the ticket pricing problem. Several options quickly came to mind. My favorite was to provide a government subsidy to the 5:00 P.M. moviegoers to allow them (that is, me) to better afford to pay more. Under this scheme the theater operator could then raise the 5:00 P.M. price to reflect full costs and lower the price to the 8:00 P.M. moviegoers who have been paying more than their "fair share." This struck me as a win-win-win situation. I win because I get the subsidy. The evening moviegoers win because they pay less.

---

1. Economists may go to more than their share of mediocre movies. For a delightful essay on movie theater pricing see: Steven E. Landsburg, "Why Popcorn Costs More at the Movies and Why the Obvious Answer Is Wrong," in *The Armchair Economist: Economics and Everyday Life* (New York: The Free Press, 1993), pp. 157–167.

1

The theater operator wins because with only one price her administrative costs are reduced.

Most people are not surprised that those attending movies in the late afternoon can get a price break. As far as I know, however, few people really believe that movie theaters lose money on this pricing structure. I suspect that people generally see this as the theaters' strategy to attract some extra patrons by showing a film they already have at an off-peak time. The lower price covers the extra costs of the additional showing and makes a contribution to paying the rent. I also doubt that most people would believe that a movie theater would lower its 8:00 P.M. ticket price *because* it raised its 5:00 P.M. price. They are more likely to believe that the theater would leave its 8:00 P.M. price as it is—or raise it too.[2]

Yet people do seem to believe that hospitals and physicians cost shift in just this way. And from all appearances, people sincerely believe that cost shifting in the health care sector is rampant. Part of the problem is definitional. Cost shifting means many different things to different people, at least in part because of the strange and complex nature of health care markets. Things that do not seem possible elsewhere appear to be commonplace in health care. And part of the problem is that people are being misled. Just because different prices are charged to different payers, it does not necessarily follow that lowering the price that one party pays leads to higher prices for everybody else.

The purpose of this monograph is to analyze cost shifting in the health care setting. We will investigate its several meanings. We will examine the underlying economic principles that support and refute those meanings. We will review the empirical evidence, and we will try to straighten out the often confusing policy implications that are said to flow from cost shifting.

Cost Shifting Defined

The simplest use of the term *cost shifting* is as a descriptor for charging different prices to different groups. Medicare pays hospitals less than

---

2. It is always dangerous to assume what people may think. I would not have thought that people believed that offering lower airline fares to those with more flexibility in their schedule would be considered selling airline seats at a loss. Nor would I have believed that the higher fares charged to others were a way for airlines to "make up" for losses incurred by offering the lower-priced fares. I do believe that airlines will cover their marginal costs with those low-priced fares and charge higher prices in those markets and at those times when consumers are less price sensitive. However, others have described the airline pricing structure as an example of cost shifting. See

commercial insurers do. Preferred provider organizations (PPOs) are charged less than small indemnity health insurers. Under this definition the mere presence of price differences is understood as cost shifting. We will call this *static cost shifting* or, more correctly, *price discrimination*.

For most of the health policy discussions of cost shifting, this static definition is not very helpful. In fact, it can be terribly misleading. It is commonly asserted, for example, that those paying the lower price actually are paying less than the true costs of the service or product. This may be so, but it need not be. The textbook economic theory of price discrimination, for example, leads to different prices paid by different buyers. According to the textbook theory, the seller adjusts the price (and thus the quantity) to each buyer so that the price just covers the cost of providing the last unit of service demanded by the buyer. Some pay higher prices, though, in part because the other buyers pay *as much* (rather than as little) as they do. The implication of the static cost shifting view of the world is that the provider is worse off because she provides care to the group paying the lower prices. In the price discrimination view, the provider is better off providing care to both groups rather than to only one. The further problem with the static cost shifting definition from a policy perspective, is that it provides no insight into what would happen if one payer began to pay less (or more).

This problem leads to the second common use of the term cost shifting. It is behavioral. Cost shifting occurs when providers raise prices to one group of payers *because* another group of payers is now paying less. I call this *dynamic cost shifting* or simply *cost shifting*. As we will see, the usual profit-maximizing behavior typically ascribed to firms by economists does not result in cost shifting. In fact, it implies just the opposite; if one is forced to lower the price to one payer, profit maximization leads the firm to lower its price to other payers as well.

One can construct a story of behaviors that lead to dynamic cost shifting; however, it requires health care market conditions and assumptions about provider choices that both limit the extent of cost shifting and suggest that it is increasingly less of a real concern.

Cost shifting of either the static or the dynamic kind usually has been applied only to hospitals. Increasingly it is being applied to physicians and nursing homes. My dentist even has a sign posted in her examining rooms encouraging patients to give to a fund for dental

---

Allen Dobson and James Roney, *Cost Shifting: A Self Limiting Process* (Washington, D.C.: Lewin-ICF, April 1992), p. 4.

care for the poor because it will allow her (ultimately) to keep her prices low.

Employers too are said to suffer because of cost shifting. Usually it is said that employers pay higher medical care prices and ultimately higher health insurance premiums because medical care providers engage in cost shifting. A newer wrinkle is that (typically) large employers who provide health insurance are the victims of cost shifting by (typically) small employers who do not offer coverage. Medical care costs of the small firm's workers are shifted to the large firm through the coverage of spouses and dependents covered under the large employer's insurance plan. This new use has its own conceptual problems, which we will discuss.

Policy Significance of Cost Shifting

Given the variety of definitions of cost shifting and implications that have been drawn from the belief that cost shifting is prevalent in the health care industry, it is not surprising that cost shifting has played an important role in the health policy debate. All manner of claims have been made:

• Errors in setting federal hospital payment rules have been of little consequence because cost shifting allows hospitals to recoup their losses.

> Currently, the impact of design flaws and use of inappropriate or erroneous data in PPS [the Medicare Prospective Payment System] is limited by the fact that affected hospitals can respond to the Federal government's payment levels by raising their charges.[3]

• Reductions in federal Medicare or Medicaid payments do not control health care costs.

> Moreover, some argue that any additional Medicare cuts made outside the realm of the health-care overhaul plan will only heighten the problem of 'cost shifting,' where doctors boost private-sector fees to make up for low government reimbursement rates. 'So really, this does very little in containing overall costs,' said Ron Pollack, executive director of

---

3. Prospective Payment Assessment Commission, *Optional Hospital Payment Rates*, Congressional Report C-92-03 (Washington, D.C., March 1992), p. 28.

Families USA, a consumer group pushing for health care revision.[4]

• Cost shifting has forced many small employers out of the insurance market.

Small employers, by nature of their size, lack leverage in the health care market. They are unable to evade the cost shift by entering into negotiated care contracts. They are, therefore, compelled to purchase indemnity policies and accept lofty premium increases. Worse, they can be forced to abandon their coverage, thus producing more uninsured patients.[5]

Officials working on the [Clinton] administration's plan bristle at the suggestion that anyone will lose. They insist that by requiring all employers to contribute to their workers' coverage, they will be putting a stop to the distortions and inequities that push up costs in the current system. Specifically, they argue, it will no longer be necessary for hospitals and doctors to overcharge those who do have insurance to pay for those who don't. The result, they contend, is that employers who now offer very generous health benefits will be able to afford to continue to do so.[6]

• Physicians should charge the same prices to all patients for the same services.

Families USA's Mr. Pollack says physicians often charge deep-pocketed insurance companies more to make up for patients and procedures covered by less generous government programs. That is why he advocates price lists pinpointing exactly how much a particular treatment will cost anyone, anytime.[7]

---

4. Hilary Stout and Rick Wartzman, "Moynihan's Proposed Medicare Cuts Could Backfire by Forcing New Taxes," *Wall Street Journal*, June 8, 1993, p. A3.

5. Sidney Marchasin, "Cost Shifting: How One Hospital Does It," *Wall Street Journal*, December 9, 1991, p. A14.

6. Rick Wartzman, "Who Wins and Who Loses under Health Plan May Be the Key to Success of Clinton's Reforms," *Wall Street Journal*, May 26, 1993, p. A20.

7. Wendy Bounds, "Sick of Skyrocketing Costs, Patients Defy Doctors and Shop for Cheaper Treatment," *Wall Street Journal*, June 16, 1993, p. B1. It is worth noting that the implicit policy suggestion here is not only that prices be posted, but also that providers be prevented from offering lower or higher prices.

- Medicare and Medicaid payment levels should be raised.

  Hospital officials say they need the revenue to make up for people who can't pay, or can't pay the full cost of service. The federal government sets the payment for services such as blood tests to Medicare patients. But that may not cover the hospital's cost. That's also true, hospital officials say, for Medicaid and indigent care. . . . This leads to "cost shifting," which means patients who can pay pick up part of the tab for those who can't.[8]

- Nursing homes should be required to charge the same price to public and private payers.

  [Federal Reserve Bank of Boston economist Jane] Little's analysis data indicate that in most states, the one-third of private nursing-home residents who aren't eligible for medicaid are actually paying for 20% to 30% of the long term care received by medicaid patients. Such cost shifting, Little argues, is inherently unfair and counterproductive. By increasing the already heavy burdens of those private payers who are unfortunate enough to require such care themselves, the practice hastens the painful day when they exhaust their savings and move onto medicaid. . . . A better policy . . . would be for states to require nursing homes to charge public and private payers the same rates. . . . They also would make it easier for regulators to spot inefficiencies and curb the explosive rise in medicaid spending.[9]

- Providing health insurance to all will save money for those employers who currently offer health insurance. Providers will no longer have to charge such high prices to pay for care to the uninsured.

  The administration is sure to make the case that by bringing down health costs, big business will win big. Officials note that companies offering health plans to their workers already pay for treating uninsured people because hospitals and doctors increase their fees to cover them. Some companies, in fact, estimate that such "cost shifting" accounts for more than 25% of their health bills.[10]

---

8. Richard Maschel, "The High Cost of a Hospital Stay," *Birmingham News*, July 12, 1993, p. 1E.

9. Gene Koretz, "Why Cost-Shifting at Nursing Homes Hurts Everyone," *Business Week*, October 5, 1992, p. 30.

10. Hilary Stout and Rick Wartzman, "With Health-Care Package Nearing Completion, Clinton Now Must Make Some Tough Decisions," *Wall Street Journal*, May 18, 1993, p. A20.

Q: I like my health insurance. Why should I pay to insure others?
A: Like now, you'll be paying to insure yourself and you'll also be getting the peace of mind that, if you lose your job or get sick, you won't lose your insurance. And remember: right now, you and your company are paying for the people who don't pay for their own health care. That's why you get charged $20 for a Tylenol when you go to the hospital. Because for every person like you who pays the bill, there's another person who will never see a bill—and couldn't pay it if they did.[11]

• Employers who do not offer health insurance have a competitive advantage over those who do, because those who do not offer insurance are able to hire workers who can obtain insurance through a spouse or parent.

The manufacturers add that they have also been hit from another quarter—by charges from their employees' spouses and other dependents, who often work in service industries or for smaller companies, where health benefits are often skimpy or nonexistent.[12]

Q: What will happen to businesses that provide insurance? Will their costs go up?
A: For many businesses, costs will actually go down. And over time, by getting health costs under control, we'll stop the chilling effect that exploding health care costs have on businesses. Right now, businesses that cover their employees are paying for those that don't. That's not fair. The Clinton plan is based on fairness and responsibility. Every employer has to take responsibility for covering their employees—giving them the security that they will never lose their insurance.[13]

However, some news reports suggest that cost shifting is not all that the policy advocates and commentators claim it is. For example:

• It is becoming more and more difficult to shift costs.

But as Dr. Johnson's experience shows, more and more private payers are cutting their own deals, leaving the brunt of the cost shifts to small employers, the self-employed and

11. *Health Care Reform: Question and Answers,* provided by the Clinton administration for the June 1993 congressional recess.
12. Milt Freudenheim, "Companies' Costs: How Much Is Fair?" *New York Times,* January 7, 1992, p. C2.
13. *Health Care Reform: Question and Answers.*

others without bargaining power. "It's become increasingly difficult to find anyone left to cost-shift to," says Fred Graefe, a lawyer and lobbyist who represents a number of health-care clients.[14]

But the golden era may end for many hospitals. Many are already being forced by employers and insurers to give up the lucrative practice of submitting jumbo bills listing hundreds of difficult-to-monitor services. Now, rather than charging for each pill, injection and service, "well over 80 percent of hospitals" are paid either a fixed daily fee or a preset amount for each illness treated, Mr. Willis of Aetna said.[15]

• Hospitals have been laying off staff, a practice that would seem to be unnecessary if cost shifting were easy to achieve.

In Boston, hospitals are weighing or implementing layoffs or reducing their staffs through attrition. Five hospitals are talking about merging. In the Twin Cities, hospitals report hiring freezes and layoffs. In Sacramento, Mercy Health Care–Sacramento just said it will cut 93 of its 5,100 jobs this summer. . . . Pittsburgh's Shadyside Hospital cut 140 positions, or 3 percent of its staff. The University of Pittsburgh Medical Center in early June eliminated 500 positions, while South Hills Health System cut 25 of 2,800 jobs and Forbes Health System has cut a total of 167 positions.[16]

• There is even an open question as to whether hospitals ever could cost shift.

But, he [Donald A. Young, executive director of the Prospective Payment Assessment Commission] said, these numbers did not prove that the Government squeeze on hospitals had actually caused the increased charges to private payers. "The literature and other things suggest that hospitals would have charged more anyhow, to maximize revenues, even if Medicare and Medicaid were paying 100 percent of hospital costs.[17]

---

14. Hilary Stout, "Health-Care Reform Must Undo Reductions in Medicare Spending," *Wall Street Journal*, August 9, 1993, p. A4.

15. Milt Freudenheim, "Hospitals Begin Streamlining for a New World in Health Care," *New York Times*, June 20, 1993, p. F12.

16. Dana Milbank, "Health Care No Longer Panacea for Cities," *Wall Street Journal*, July 13, 1993, p. A2.

17. Freudenheim, "Companies' Costs: How Much Is Fair?" p. C2.

What Is the Evidence?

This wide range of allegations gives rise to the natural question: How many of them are true? There are three fundamental issues. First, do providers charge different prices to different payers? Yes, they do. The evidence, particularly with respect to hospitals, is clear. Medicaid and Medicare pay lower prices than most privately insured patients do.

Second, are these differences justified on the basis of differences in the actual costs of providing service? Here the evidence is less definitive. The weight of the hospital evidence suggests that costs per day are about equal for all categories of payers. Medicare patients tend to have longer lengths of stay for the same diagnoses, however, and Medicaid and uninsured patients tend to use hospitals that are more costly. These differences imply that the average cost of treating Medicare patients, at least, is higher—not lower—than that of treating other patients. The real issue, however, revolves around marginal, not average, costs. Here the evidence is lacking. Further, there is little evidence available about differences in the cost of physician services.

Third, and most important, do providers raise prices to some payers *because* other payers pay less? That is, is there dynamic cost shifting? The economics suggest that this is unlikely. Under the usual economic assumptions shifting costs is not a rational thing to do. One can construct conditions under which it makes good sense to shift costs—for example, when providers "favor" private paying patients and, therefore, have not been charging them all they profitably could have. The empirical evidence on hospitals is mixed, at best. Two studies find evidence of less-than-complete cost shifting and argue that there are significant limits on its use. Two other studies find no evidence of cost shifting. There has been only one study of dynamic cost shifting among physicians. Although it finds evidence of cost shifting, this evidence is better characterized as evidence of changes in utilization.

Finally, do employers face higher insurance costs because they cover the spouses and dependents of workers employed by firms that do not offer insurance? The economics suggest that there is no cost shifting of this sort. The relevant issue is not health insurance per se, but total costs. The argument is that wages adjust to reflect higher or lower levels of health insurance. This turns out to be a very difficult argument to address empirically. Early efforts found little evidence of wage adjustments; however, more recent sophisticated research on pensions, workers' compensation insurance, and health insurance

9

provides rather dramatic evidence that wages do adjust. The lower wages paid by those employers providing insurance counters the assertions of cost-shifting from employers without insurance to employers with insurance.

Road Map to the Book

Chapter 2 discusses the economics of charging different prices to different payers and the implications of one payer's paying less. It focuses on three alternative approaches to health care pricing. All lead to static cost shifting; only one leads to dynamic cost shifting. Chapter 3 presents the evidence on whether hospitals and physicians actually charge different prices. Chapter 4 examines the extent to which there are cost differences among payers. An easy explanation for different prices is that sicker patients or patients who otherwise require more services cost more. Chapter 5 examines the empirical evidence on hospitals' and physicians' ability to raise prices to one group in response to price reductions by another. Chapter 6 explores the growing evidence of price competition in hospital markets. Under any of the pricing models, static and dynamic cost shifting requires the provider to have market power—the ability to freely set prices. In the presence of price competition this freedom is limited by the market. Chapter 7 examines cost shifting in the employment setting. Here the issues revolve around the nature of labor compensation. Shifting occurs, but in the *form* of compensation, not costs. Finally, Chapter 8 revisits the claims that cost shifting is prevalent—and is successful—in light of the available evidence. It then examines the implications of various policy prescriptions.

2
The Economics of Cost Shifting

Cost shifting implies the ability to successfully set different prices for different categories of payers. The ability to do this requires market power on the part of the hospital. Without it there is no tale to tell. If a hospital without market power tried to raise its price to any given category of payers, the buyers would go elsewhere, and the attempt to raise prices would be unsuccessful.

We will define *static cost shifting* as a hospital or other provider's ability to charge different prices to different payers. This is better called *price discrimination*. Evidence that different payers pay different prices is easy to establish, as we shall see in the next chapter.

Dynamic cost shifting means something more. Cost shifting is said to be dynamic when a provider lowers (or raises) the price charged to one payer and in turn charges other payers more (or less). This is much harder to establish both conceptually and empirically. The conceptual difficulty comes as a provider trys to raise his price. The usual model used by economists to describe the behavior of firms is *profit maximization*. Simply put, it means charging all that the traffic will bear. This does not mean the highest possible price because, as the price is increased, people will buy less. Over some range the higher price more than offsets the reduced volume of sales. Eventually, however, a still higher price is overwhelmed by a disproportionally larger reduction in volume. The firm will have killed (or at least badly wounded) the golden goose.

In this view a hospital with two markets will set prices in each so as to extract all the profit each market can bear.[1] Suppose that for some reason one market will no longer pay its price, perhaps because a new provider has entered that market or the local government has lowered the legal price. The hospital may be tempted to try to raise the price in the other market to "recoup" the loss. But this turns out to be impossible to do successfully. In fact, as we demonstrate below, the profit-maximizing response is to shift *capacity* to the other market

---

1. If possible, and assuming hospital services cannot be bought in one market and sold in the other. See below.

and sell the service at a lower, not higher, price. The usual economic assumptions do not lead to dynamic cost shifting as it is typically defined in the health policy literature.

It turns out that dynamic cost shifting requires a hospital to have not only market power, but *unexploited* market power. That is, the hospital must have the ability to charge one category of payers a higher price (consistent with higher profits), even though, so far, it has chosen not to do so. Unexploited market power, in turn has two necessary conditions: (1) The hospital, or more precisely, the hospital's decision makers, must value something other than profits exclusively;[2] (2) one of the things it values must be the group that is cost shifted against; that is, it must value privately insured patients. This last point is crucial. The hospital does not value private patients because they pay their bills; rather, because the hospital "favors" private patients, it charges them less than it profitably could. Without these conditions dynamic cost shifting is not possible.

This chapter begins with a discussion of a simple profit-maximizing hospital. The hospital has market power and two categories of payers. We discuss the setting of prices in the two markets. Then we analyze what would happen if one payer, the government, began to pay less. This is followed by a discussion of a hospital that values things other than profit. We will see that valuing perquisites for the administration and the medical staff, or valuing government or uninsured indigent patients, has the same implications for privately insured patients that profit maximization does. There is no dynamic cost shifting. Finally, see what happens when a hospital "favors" privately paying patients. In this scenario, when the government lowers its payment level, the hospital raises its price to private payers, just as the theory of dynamic cost shifting would suggest.

The Simple, Greedy, Profit-Maximizing Hospital

Almost everyone has seen the movie *It's a Wonderful Life* with Jimmy Stewart and Donna Reed. In it old man Potter is the richest man in Bedford Falls. At one point in the movie Potter says to the hero, George Bailey: "You know just as I do that I run practically everything

---

2. See, Mark Pauly and Michael Redisch, "The Not-for-Profit Hospital as a Physician Cooperative," *American Economic Review*, vol. 63, no. 1 (March 1973), pp. 87–99; Jeffrey E. Harris, "The Internal Organization of Hospitals: Some Economic Implications," *Bell Journal of Economics* (Autumn 1977), pp. 467–82; Joseph P. Newhouse, "Toward a Theory of Nonprofit Institutions: An Economic Model of a Hospital," *American Economic Review*, vol. 60, no. 1 (March 1970), pp. 64–74.

in town but the Bailey Building and Loan." Suppose he owned the only hospital, and it was a very long way to another town. Suppose, too, that the hospital had two kinds of patients: those who could pay and those who were covered by the government. My apologies to Frank Capra.

The government pays the Potter Hospital a fixed price per admission. Those who can pay have a downward sloping demand curve. This means that at a lower price they would buy more hospital care. This is not so strange. The Rand Health Insurance Experiment found that people who were fully insured used 29 percent more hospital admissions per year than those who had to pay virtually the full price.[3] The complete insurance coverage lowered the out-of-pocket price to zero, and people consumed more.[4]

Given that the hospital is to continue operations, Potter has to face two questions: (1) Does he accept government patients? and (2) What price does he charge to privately insured patients?[5] The answers are standard fare in a business economics or intermediate microeconomic theory course, so they are second nature to Potter. The object is to extract as much profit from each market as possible. In the government market Potter would admit patients and continue to do so until the additional revenue generated by an admission is just equal to the extra costs. Admitting more patients would mean that the last ones cost more to treat than the revenue they generated. Potter would not stand for that. Admitting fewer would mean giving up patients who generate more revenue than costs. Potter wouldn't do that either.

When Potter tries to follow this rule in the private market, he faces a dilemma. The problem is that he can charge only a single price

---

3. Willard G. Manning et al., "Health Insurance and the Demand for Medical Care: Evidence from a Randomized Experiment," *American Economic Review*, vol. 77, no. 3 (June 1987), pp. 251–77.

4. The fact that people buy more health services when prices are lower may be key to understanding the cost shifting debate. If one believes that people buy the same amount of health services regardless of price, then hospital pricing rules appear arbitrary and cost shifting has a life virtually independent of markets. However, there is substantial evidence that people do buy less health care when faced with higher prices. See chapter 6, and Michael A. Morrisey, *Price Sensitivity in Health Care: Implications for Health Care Policy*, (Washington: NFIB Foundation, 1992).

5. Potter doesn't dislike doing business with the government. When World War II came to Bedford Falls, we fully expect that Potter's manufacturing concerns would be characterized by wartime profiteering. An interesting side question is why Potter ran the local draft board.

FIGURE 2–1
PRICING AT POTTER HOSPITAL

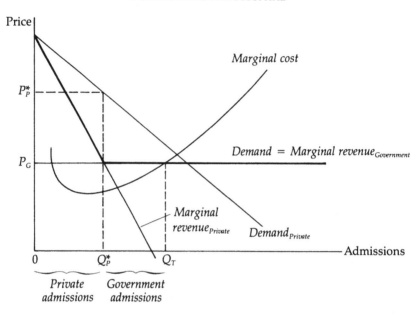

SOURCE: Author.

per admission to all private patients.[6] Lowering his price to attract more admissions means that he also must lower his price to people who would have paid more. So he must find a price where the additional revenue, net of these price reductions, is equal to the additional cost of treating the additional patients.

And there is an additional kicker. The relevant cost to Potter is the higher of two costs: the actual cost of providing the care, or the amount that the government would pay for one of its patients. In the choice between admitting a publicly or a privately insured patient, Potter would accept the one who yielded the more profit. So, at every point Potter must calculate the projected revenue from each source and the extra cost of providing services. Put differently, Potter will continue to admit patients until the marginal revenue from private patients is equal to the marginal revenue from government patients and is equal to the marginal cost of providing services.

---

6. On this point maybe it is easiest to assume that those who can pay are insured by a preferred provider organization, which has negotiated a fixed charge per admission. Either way, the story remains the same.

14

Figure 2-1 presents this logic graphically. The hospital views the government price (P_G) as given and can admit all the government patients it chooses to at this price. Because the government price does not change with volume, the government price and the government marginal revenue are equal. Private payers have a downward sloping demand curve (*Demand*$_{Private}$). Because of this, each lower price draws more patients into the hospital, but it also results in less revenue per patient. This is reflected by the *Marginal revenue*$_{Private}$ curve. Private and government patients are equally costly, but eventually more patients of either category result in higher service costs, so the marginal cost curve is eventually upward sloping.

The dark kinked line is the envelope of marginal revenue. It traces out the maximum possible additional revenue attainable if one carefully chooses the patients paying the most at any point. Notice that eventually the government-insured patients generate more marginal revenue than additional privately insured patients.

Potter maximizes profits by producing Q_T admissions. This is where the envelope of marginal revenue equals marginal cost. He then distributes the capacity across the payer categories by setting the price in the private market. Privately insured patients will get Q_P admissions and will have to pay price P_P. The government patients will get Q_T minus Q_P admissions at the P_G price.[7]

Two important observations emerge from this exercise. First, Potter will charge different prices to the two categories of payers. Economists call this third-degree price discrimination. We will also call it static cost shifting. Only three things are required to price discriminate successfully. First, one must have market power. Second, one must have categories of payers that have different degrees of price sensitivity. Third, one must have the ability to keep people in the lower-priced markets from reselling to those in the higher-priced markets. Preventing resale is pretty easy to accomplish in health care, although Potter must be careful that government patients do not loan out their government cards, and he does not want the government

---

7. Notice that Potter could face several different classes of payers. As long as they have different degrees of price sensitivity and cannot resell the admissions, he will find the profit-maximizing price for each. For a discussion of textbook price discrimination, see Donald S. Watson, *Price Theory and Its Uses* (Boston: Houghton Mifflin Co., 1968), pp. 324–36. For applications to hospitals, see Joel Hay, "The Impact of Public Health Care Financing Policies on Private Sector Hospital Costs," *Journal of Health Politics, Policy and Law*, vol. 7, no. 4 (Winter 1983), pp. 945–52; and Richard Foster, "Cost-Shifting under Cost Reimbursement and Prospective Payment," *Journal of Health Economics*, vol. 4, no. 3 (1985), pp. 261–71.

plan to cover people who otherwise would have been privately insured. Indeed, Reuben Kessel argued that the reason for physicians' initial opposition to health insurance was precisely this concern. The insurance plan would result in lower payments from people who could have paid more.[8]

Differing price sensitivity means that the markets have different responses to prices. This typically means better or worse access to substitute sources of care. Those with better substitute sources will pay lower prices. If one group of privately insured patients could use a hospital serving only members of a local lodge but other privately insured patients could not, for example, Potter would set a lower price for the lodge members. In Potter's case, the government has set a price. If the hospital charged a lower price, it would attract no more patients than with the established price; a higher price would yield no patients at all.

Market power merely means that at least one category of payers faces a downward sloping demand curve from the point of view of the hospital. The hospital will not lose all its patients if it raises its prices.

A second important observation is that, although costs play an important part in determining the capacity of the hospital and the prices that Mr. Potter sets, government-insured patients are not being treated at a loss. If he were losing money on them, Potter could do better by not selling to government patients and focusing exclusively on the private payers. The easiest way to see this is to note that the marginal revenue from the government over the range Q_P to Q_T lies everywhere above both the marginal cost curve and the marginal revenue curve of private payers. It is true that private payers pay more because there are government-insured patients in Bedford Falls.[9] But this is not because the government pays so little; it is because it pays so much. The government-insured patients effectively bid capacity away from the private market.

The essence of the dynamic cost-shifting argument is that when the government lowers its price, people in the private market are said to have to pay more. If the Roosevelt administration had done this in Potter's time, how would Potter have responded to maximize profits?

The answer is straightforward. Let the government set a still-lower price per admission. Some of the hospital's government admissions now cost more than the revenue they generate. Potter would

---

8. Reuben A. Kessel, "Price Discrimination in Medicine," *Journal of Law and Economics*, vol. 1, no. 1 (1958), pp. 20–53.

9. If there were only privately insured patients Potter would maximize profits by selling quantity Q_p^* in figure 2–1 at price P_p^*.

FIGURE 2–2
Response of Potter Hospital to Government Price Cut

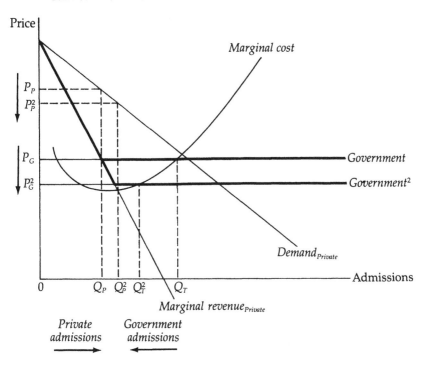

SOURCE: Author.

not allow that. He would reduce the number of admissions available to government patients and shift some of the capacity over to the private market. Unfortunately for Potter, the private market will buy more only if the price is reduced. This is reverse cost shifting! It is easily seen in figure 2–2. Figure 2–2 replicates figure 2–1 but adds a second, lower, government payment line, P_G^2. If one conducts the same exercise with the new government price, it is clear that total output is reduced somewhat, from Q_T to Q_T^2, government capacity is reduced from (Q_T minus Q_P) to (Q_T^2 minus Q_P^2), private capacity is expanded from Q_P to Q_P^2. The only way to unload this capacity is to cut the private price, from P_P to P_P^2.

Thus, a self-respecting, profit-maximizing hospital with market power will respond to a cut in the government payment level by *lowering the price to private payers*. The same economic principles work in the opposite direction. Suppose Potter's lobbyists in Washington

17

were able to get the government to raise the price it pays for hospital services. The hospital would find government-insured patients more attractive and would seek to admit more of them. Hospital capacity would grow a bit. In addition, the hospital would find that the opportunity cost of admitting a privately insured patient had risen. Admitting a private patient means that a better-paying Medicare patient does not get in. So, Potter's hospital would raise the price to private patients when the government raised its payment level.

The moral of the Potter Hospital story is that a profit-maximizing hospital will charge different prices to different categories of payers, but it will not engage in dynamic cost shifting. Rather than charging private payers more because the government pays less, Potter Hospital would charge private payers less when the government pays less, and more when the government pays more.

The More Complex Utility-Maximizing Hospital

Suppose that a nonprofit community trust owns the Bedford Falls Hospital, instead of Mr. Potter. Suppose that the trust appointed George Bailey to run the hospital. George, as you recall, was a man full of ideas. He wants the hospital to be the best. It should be a high-quality hospital and look like one. It should offer high-quality services and have a happy and dedicated medical staff. It should be called the Bedford Falls Medical Center.

Now it should be pointed out that old man Potter was no sentimentalist; if these things had paid, he would have put them in the hospital when it was his. So George has the challenge of providing these good things to people who don't want to pay for them. The hospital has no particular endowment that it can use. George must rely on surpluses from operations.

If the Medical Center is to be all it can be, George Bailey must generate all the surplus he can to pay for the improvements. Surplus, of course, is just another word for profit. George quickly discovers the maxim of nonprofit hospital success: "No margin, no mission." The business problem is identical to that faced by Potter. If the Bedford Falls Medical Center is to prosper it must charge all that the traffic will bear in each of its markets. George Bailey will price discriminate; he will engage in static cost shifting. The only difference between old man Potter's profit-maximizing hospital and George's hospital is how they spend the proceeds.

Not surprisingly, if the government does cut its level of payment, George will be forced to do just what Potter did: reduce admissions of government-insured patients and shift capacity to the private market—resulting in a reduction in the private price.

Suppose George had discovered another category of patients in Bedford Falls, those unable to pay for care. He would seek to generate as much surplus from both categories of insured patients as he could and spend those profits on the uninsured poor. If there were suddenly more poor, there would be nothing George could do. There is no extra profit that he can coax out of his paying patients. If he were able to get more, he would not have been maximizing his surplus to begin with.[10]

Two other implications for Bedford Falls Medical Center are worth noting. First, if the government were to cut its payment level, the medical center would both cut its price to private payers (because doing so salvages as much remaining surplus as possible) and reduce its level of charity care (because it has less total surplus to spend on the poor).

Second, suppose the government were to pay the hospital for the care it has been providing for the poor. One could think of this as a simple health care reform plan. What would happen to the prices charged to private payers? The answer depends on what things are valued by George Bailey and the board of the Medical Center. To the extent that they are committed to the quality and image that I described at the beginning of this section, we should see no change in private prices. The nonprofit hospital has other services it wishes to provide besides care for the indigent. These are best accomplished by charging the surplus- or profit-maximizing price.

The lesson of the Bedford Falls Medical Center is that simply having objectives other than profit maximization still leads the hospital to charge different prices to different payers. The hospital continues to practice static cost shifting but not dynamic cost shifting. When the government cuts its level of reimbursement, the hospital *reduces* its price to paying patients. Contrary to the view of dynamic cost shifting, it does not raise private prices.

Getting to Dynamic Cost Shifting

Suppose that the nonprofit Bedford Falls Medical Center continues to have market power but that private patients are among the things it

---

10. This may explain why the proportion of "self-paying" patients at general community hospitals remained stable during the 1980s as the number of uninsured grew. The increased numbers of uninsured were treated in the large urban public hospitals, which had access to tax dollars for charity care. See Frank A. Sloan, Michael A. Morrisey, and Joseph Valvona, "Hospital Care for the 'Self-Pay' Patient," *Journal of Health Politics, Policy and Law*, vol. 13, no. 1 (Spring 1988), pp. 83–102.

values. Old man Potter valued private patients for the revenue they generated. The Medical Center values them in the sense that it "favors" them. It plans to charge them less than the profit- or surplus-maximizing price. Potter would describe the hospital as having unexploited monopoly power.[11]

Again think of the Medical Center with two categories of patients: the government and privately insured. These markets are just as described before. One way to think of the Medical Center's pricing problem is to think of the hospital as calculating the profit-maximizing prices it could set and the quantities it would provide to each, just as Potter (and George Bailey) did. The hospital now, however, spends the profits on more privately insured patients. It backs off the profit-maximizing price for private patients and charges them less than it could have.[12]

Given the cost structure that we set up in the earlier examples, the hospital will still engage in static cost shifting; that is, it will still charge a different price to each category of payers. It will charge private patients more than it charges the government.

Now consider what happens when the government cuts its level of reimbursement. The lower payment rate means that government patients generate less surplus. Therefore, the hospital has less revenues with which to subsidize its private patients. It must now spend less on "underpricing" and raise its prices to private patients. This is dynamic cost shifting.[13]

Dynamic cost shifting—the practice of raising prices to one category of payer when another pays less—is successful when private

---

11. It is tempting to let George's kind but daft Uncle Billy run the hospital under this scenario, but that would be unfair. Other commentators have characterized the hospital board as not permitting charges to be set at levels above those "needed to provide quality." This could be construed as "favoring" privately insured patients. See Paul Ginsburg and Kenneth Thorpe, "All-Payer Rate Setting and the Competitive Strategy," *Health Affairs*, vol. 11, no. 2 (Summer 1992), pp. 73–87.

12. There is no reason for the hospital to back off the government price, in our example, since the federal government has set this rate. One could imagine the hospital wishing to provide more services to these patients—services that the government program will not pay for. This, however, is just an example of the George Bailey–run hospital that we analyzed above. In this scenario the rule is to set the surplus-maximizing private price and spend the profits on more services to government patients.

13. For an elegant exposition of this theory, see David Dranove, "Pricing By Non-Profit Institutions," *Journal of Health Economics*, vol. 7, no. 1 (March 1988), pp. 47–57.

patients have been paying prices lower than the profit-maximizing price. The hospital can move these prices back up toward the profit-maximizing level.

There are limits to dynamic cost shifting. If the hospital were to continue to raise its prices to privately insured patients, it would ultimately reach the profit-maximizing level. Once that occurs, attempts to raise prices further would lead to large enough reductions in the number of private patients, which would in turn result in less, not more, revenue. Once this point is reached, even this hospital must respond to government price reductions in the same manner as the Potter- and George Bailey–run hospitals did. It must then cut private prices in the face of the government payment reductions.

Summary

In price-competitive health care markets there would be no price discrimination or cost shifting of either the static or the dynamic variety. Attempts to raise prices to one category of payers would induce them to seek care elsewhere. Cost shifting requires that health care providers have market power.

Price discrimination or static cost shifting is easy to establish, at least conceptually. It results from differing degrees of price sensitivity across payer groups. We used the example of government-insured and privately insured patients. One would expect, however, to see different prices for two groups of privately insured patients if one group has better substitute sources of care. The group with greater price sensitivity will pay the lower price.

Dynamic cost shifting, or raising the price to one group in response to a price cut to another group, is much more difficult to establish. A profit-maximizing firm would not do it. This sort of provider would try to shift *capacity* from the now lower-paying market to the higher-paying market. To sell the added capacity in this market the firm must lower its price. Thus, an attempt by, say, Medicare or a large insurer to get a lower price does not lead to higher prices for other payers. It results in lower prices to them.

Even a hospital that values things besides profits will not engage in dynamic cost shifting. Since it wants to provide as many of these other things as possible, it will rationally charge the profit-maximizing price in each of its markets and use these profits (or surpluses) to pay for the things its board values. This sort of provider will find dynamic cost shifting inconsistent with its mission.

Dynamic cost shifting exists when the provider values a particular class of paying patients. The surpluses are spent, in part, on lower prices for this favored group. When an unfavored patient category is able to negotiate a lower price, the provider finds that she has less surplus and is forced to raise prices for the favored patient category to something closer to the profit-maximizing level.

There are limits to dynamic cost shifting. As the provider is forced to raise prices, she ultimately approaches the profit-maximizing level. Once this happens dynamic cost shifting ceases. This provider is forced to act like those in the other models.

Just as there is in Capra's *It's a Wonderful Life*, there has been a certain otherworldliness about the discussion in this chapter. The repeated suggestion that hospitals might lower their prices in response to higher government payments seems wholly inconsistent with experience. But we have assumed away any true differences in the costs of providing services to different categories of patients, and we have ignored the myriad complexities in the industry. We will use the real world to confront these theories in the following chapters. As a preview, keep in mind a comment made to me by a Blue Cross executive from Florida concerning the distinction between hospitals' charges and the prices actually paid by Blue Cross: "I love it when hospitals raise their charges; all it means is that I can show my clients how much more I have saved them."

3
Do Hospitals and Physicians Charge Different Prices?

The easiest way to think about hospital prices is to think about new car prices or airline fares. In each instance the provider of the product or service sets a high nominal price, but large segments of the population pay less, often much less. In this chapter we first review the evidence on differential pricing by hospitals and physicians. Hospitals do charge different prices to different payers. Static cost shifting or price discrimination appears to exist. I say appears to exist because one explanation for price differentials is differences in the costs of care. We explore the cost issue in detail in the next chapter. The evidence for differential pricing by physicians is much less well documented, but the story is the same. Different payers appear to pay different prices. Indeed, one of the first published articles in the comparatively new field of health economics was entitled "Price Discrimination in Medicine."[1]

In this chapter we also examine the trends in prices listed by hospitals and those actually negotiated by them. The data show diverging trends. Hospital list prices have been rising much more rapidly than actual transaction prices. We will discuss the nature of hospital and physician contracts with health maintenance organizations (HMOs) and preferred provider organizations (PPOs). A hint of the gap between what providers say they charge and what they actually agree to accept as payment was given by a representative of the Michigan Hospital Association back in 1989. "Charges are pretty meaningless. Posted charges are paid only by a very small proportion of patients."[2]

Hospital Prices

Hospitals routinely establish a price list for their services. These prices are called "full billed charges" or simply "charges." In the previous

---

1. Kessel, "Price Discrimination in Medicine," pp. 20–53.
2. D. Mayer, "Hospitals Facing Greater Pressure to Release Prices," *HealthWeek*, no. 3 (1989), p. 24.

FIGURE 3-1
AVERAGE HOSPITAL TRANSACTION PRICES, 1990

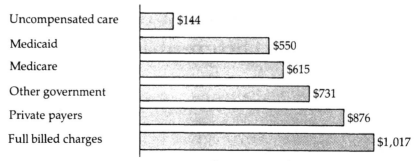

Payment per day

SOURCE: Calculated from Prospective Payment Assessment Commission, *Optional Hospital Payment Rates*, Congressional Report C-9203 (Washington, D.C.: March 1992), p. 29; and American Hospital Payment Association, *Hospital Statistics: 1990*, Chicago, p. 21.

chapter we argued that even if it cost the same to care for different patients, the hospital with market power would find it most profitable, or most consistent with its mission, to charge different prices to different payers. In fact hospitals do charge different amounts to different categories of payers. Figure 3-1 demonstrates this.

In 1990 full billed charges per day averaged over $1,000 in short-term general acute care hospitals. Every category of payer averaged less than this rate. Private insurers, on average, paid 86 percent of full charges. Medicare, with its diagnosis related group (DRG) system of administered prices, paid $615 per day, on average, or just over 60 percent of charges. Medicaid paid 54 percent of charges. People classified under uncompensated care actually paid 14 percent of charges. Uncompensated care payments come from those who make some contribution to their hospital bill and payments for the indigent made directly by local and state governments.

More than the usual care must be taken in interpreting these numbers. First, average prices can differ for a variety of cost reasons. It could be that patients in one payer category are more severely ill. Because their days of care will be more medically intense, one would expect the hospital to charge more. What is more, if selected categories of patients disproportionately use hospitals that have higher costs, then these patients will appear to pay higher prices even though all patients within a single hospital are paying the same price. We review the cost evidence in the next chapter.

A second reason for looking skeptically at average transaction prices is that the average may mask large differences within payer categories. Medicaid is an example with easily available data. In 1989 Medicaid paid 93.5 percent of billed charges in Maryland but only 39 percent in Illinois.[3]

In discussing cost shifting, it is particularly important to look at the prices actually paid by private insurers. These are the payers who are said to be harmed by lower payments from government programs and by hospitals' provision of care for the uninsured. Unfortunately, these data are the hardest to come by and easily misinterpreted. MEDSTAT collects claims data on more than seventy-five of its very large employer clients. It reported a median hospital discount from billed charges of approximately 3 percent. The "most aggressive" one-fourth of the firms, however, reported discounts of 16 percent on average in 1990.[4]

These data are, of course, hardly representative. More bothersome, the relevant measure is not the discount but the transaction price. Hospitals have adopted different marketing strategies. In Birmingham, Alabama, for example, some hospitals are said to have established relatively low list prices and to offer only modest discounts. Others have high list prices but are reported to offer substantial discounts at the first possible opportunity. The "most aggressive" employers in the MEDSTAT sample may merely have found hospitals with high charge–large discount strategies.

Over the past two decades, we have seen enormous change in the nature of the private health insurance industry. In the mid 1970s the industry was dominated by large, vertically integrated firms: Blue Cross, Blue Shield, and large commercial insurers. Since that time there has been considerable entry into each of the components of the once-integrated health insurance firm's product. The advent of low-cost computer services meant that large carriers lost their comparative advantage in administrative services. Third-party administrators entered the field and competed for that segment of the insurer's business. By 1985 some 16 percent of insured workers in medium-sized and large private firms were covered by a health insurance plan that was self-administered or that used a third-party administrator.[5]

---

3. Prospective Payment Assessment Commission, *Medicare and the American Health Care System*, Report to the Congress (Washington, D.C., June 1992), p. 28.

4. *The MEDSTAT Report*, no. 1 (Ann Arbor, Mich. MEDSTAT Systems, Inc., 1992), pp. 8–9.

5. Gail A. Jensen and Jon R. Gabel, "The Erosion of Purchased Health Insurance," *Inquiry*, vol. 25, no. 3 (Fall 1988), pp. 328–343.

Larger, experience-rated employers also found that they were bearing much of the claims risk of their health insurance. Many of them self-insured in whole or in part and thereby entered the risk-bearing component of the market. It has been estimated that in 1990 56 percent of employees were in self-insured plans.[6] This trend was undoubtedly aided by the Employee Retirement Income Security Act (ERISA) legislation in 1974, which allowed self-insured firms to avoid state premium taxes, coverage mandates, and other regulations.[7]

More important for our purposes, this period also saw the entry of firms with an apparent comparative advantage in negotiating with providers. HMOs and PPOs grew substantially. By 1992, 17.3 percent of the U.S. population was enrolled in an HMO.[8] The forty largest PPOs had 13.2 million eligible employees, or 5.2 percent of the population.[9] Data from the Health Insurance Association of America indicate that more than 18 percent of employees with health insurance were in PPO plans in 1990.[10] This is not to suggest that large insurers have abandoned the field. Quite the contrary. They self-insure, and they are the sponsors of many of the largest HMOs and PPOs.

The point is that the nature of the private health insurance business has changed. Once a comparative advantage rested with large organizations that could do the paper processing most inexpensively. Today the comparative advantage increasingly lies with the organization that is best able to negotiate in the local health care markets.

Figure 3–2 suggests the extent to which PPOs have negotiated with local hospitals and how quickly the contracts appear to be changing. Only 6 percent of PPOs pay hospitals on the basis of usual and customary charges. Over 80 percent have negotiated discounts. The average discount is reported to be 17 percent. Seventy-one percent have per diem contracts; almost one-third have DRG-based agreements. Per diems and DRGs are the fastest growing and are less susceptible to the high charge–large discount strategies used by some hospitals.

---

6. Cynthia B. Sullivan and Thomas Rice, "The Health Insurance Picture in 1990," *Health Affairs*, vol. 10, no. 2 (Summer 1991), pp. 104–15.

7. Jon R. Gabel and Gail A. Jensen, "The Price of State Mandated Benefits," *Inquiry*, vol. 26, no. 4 (Winter 1989), pp. 419–31.

8. *Marion Merrell Dow Managed Care Digest*, HMO edition (Kansas City, Mo.: Marion Merrell Dow, Inc., 1993), p. 4.

9. *Marion Merrell Dow Managed Care Digest*, update edition (Kansas City, Mo.: Marion Merrell Dow, Inc., 1992), pp. 30–31.

10. Elizabeth W. Hoy, Richard E. Curtis, and Thomas Rice, "Change and Growth in Managed Care," *Health Affairs*, vol. 10, no. 4 (Winter 1991), pp. 18–36.

FIGURE 3–2
METHODS OF PAYING HOSPITALS BY PPOs, 1990 AND 1991

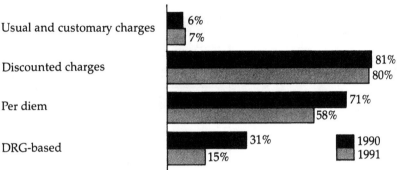

Percentage of PPOs (weighted by eligible workers)

Note: Percentages total more than 100 percent because PPOs gave multiple answers.
SOURCE: *Marion Merrell Dow Managed Care Digest*, PPO edition (Kansas City, Mo.: Marion Merrell Dow, Inc., 1992), p. 38.

The Marion Merrell Dow data in figure 3–2 may overstate the extent of payment system negotiation. PPOs typically have several hospital contracts but may concentrate their admissions in selected hospitals. Using data from eighty-two of its commercial insurer members, the Health Insurance Association of America (HIAA) found that in 1990 nearly 18 percent of insurers used billed charges as the principal method of paying hospitals. Nonetheless, they did find that 35 percent had discounts, 25 percent used per diem contracts, and 22 percent had negotiated DRG-based payments. Among HMO plans they found much greater reliance on discounts. See figure 3–3. The data are consistent, however, in suggesting that different private payers pay different prices.

It is worth noting that although PPOs and HMOs have contracts with several providers, there is evidence that at least some of these insurers more frequently use the hospitals that offer the lowest price. In a study of four metropolitan areas, Roger Feldman and colleagues found that HMOs choose hospitals on the basis of the quality of care that they provide.[11] Once chosen, however, the volume of use

11. Roger Feldman et al, "Effects of HMOs on the Creation of Competitive Markets for Hospital Services," *Journal of Health Economics*, vol. 9, no. 3 (September 1990), pp. 207–22.

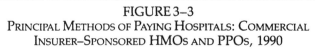

FIGURE 3–3
PRINCIPAL METHODS OF PAYING HOSPITALS: COMMERCIAL
INSURER–SPONSORED HMOs AND PPOs, 1990

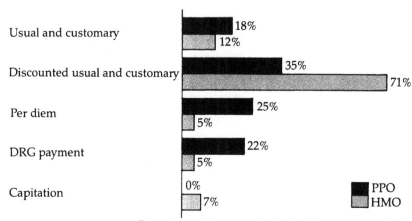

Percentage of insurers (weighted by total premium)

SOURCE: Elizabeth W. Hoy, Richard E. Curtis, and Thomas Rice, "Change and Growth in Managed Care" *Health Affairs*, vol. 10, no. 4 (Winter 1991), p. 26.

depended to a large degree on price. A 1 percent lower price negotiated with a hospital by a group- or network-model HMO was associated with a 3 percent increase in admissions at that hospital. We examine the issues of hospital and insurer competition in more detail in chapter 6.

Physician Prices

Representative physician prices are even more difficult to obtain than hospital prices. Three bits of data serve to establish that physicians do charge different transaction prices to different payer classes. The first come from the experience of the Medicare program.

Historically Medicare has paid physicians using a system based on customary, prevailing, and reasonable charges. Under this system Medicare's allowed charge was the minimum of the physician's actual, customary, and prevailing charge. Customary meant the price that the physician charged other patients for similar services, and prevailing meant a price no greater than what was charged by others in the community. Medicare now uses a fee schedule to determine its reimbursement to physicians. Under both the old system and the new a physician has the option of deciding to accept the assigned payment or not.[12]

If the physician accepts assignment, Medicare will pay the doctor directly for her services, less the Medicare beneficiary's copayment. This constitutes full payment. Or the physician may decline Medicare's assignment. In this case the patient is responsible for the doctor's full bill. Medicare pays the patient what it considers to be the reasonable payment. The patient is responsible for the copayment and any amount the physician charges over and above the Medicare-determined reasonable fee. This approach has come to be called *balance billing*. The physician effectively bills the patient for the balance of the bill not paid by Medicare. Physicians are free to decide whether to accept the Medicare assignment with each occasion of service. By 1987 Medicare paid 75.8 percent of billed charges, on average.[13]

The Health Care Financing Administration (HCFA) regularly publishes the assignment rates of participating physicians. In 1970 over 60 percent of physicians accepted assignment. By 1978 this figure had dropped to 50.5 percent. The assignment rate rose to 81.1 percent in 1990.[14] The recent increase has a lot to do with freezes on Medicare fees and limits on the extent of balance billing.[15] Further, the Medicare fee schedule places tighter limits on balance billing and provides some incentive to uniformly accept assignment for all Medicare patients. Physicians accepting assignment on all Medicare patients are now called participating providers.

For our purposes, the fact that physicians often accept assignment and sometimes do not suggests that different patients are charged different prices. The use of the term *customary* in Medicare and many Blue Shield physician contracts also suggests that different prices are potentially charged.

Surveys of physicians offer the second bit of evidence. Nineteen ninety-one data from the American Medical Association (AMA) indicate that private insurers, on average, pay prices that are 88 percent of "usual fees" and the Medicare program pays prices that are 55 percent of usual fees.[16]

---

12. See H. E. Frech III, "Overview of Policy Issues," in H. E. Frech III, ed., *Regulating Doctors' Fees*, Washington, D.C.: AEI Press, 1991, pp. 1–34.

13. Stephen Zuckerman and John Holahan, "The Role of Balance Billing in Medicare Physician Payment Reform," in ibid., pp. 143–69.

14. *EBRI Databook on Employee Benefits* (Washington, D.C.: Employee Benefit Research Institute, 1992), p. 316.

15. For a discussion, see Zuckerman and Holahan, "The Role of Balance Billing."

16. Anita J. Chawla, "Medicare and Private Insurance Reimbursement for

FIGURE 3–4
METHODS OF PAYING PHYSICIANS BY PPOS, 1991

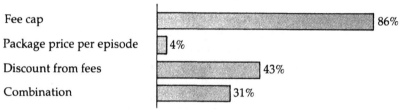

Percentage of PPOs (weighted by eligible workers)

Note: Percentages total more than 100 percent because PPOs gave multiple answers.
SOURCE: *Marion Merrell Dow Managed Care Digest*, PPO edition (Kansas City, Mo.: Marion Merrell Dow, Inc., 1992), p. 38.

The private insurance market remains the most important for our purposes. Here the available data relate to the nature of payment negotiated by PPOs and HMOs. Figure 3–4 shows that 86 percent of PPOs responding to the Marion Merrell Dow survey had instituted a fee cap that specified the maximum amount they would pay for specific services. Forty-three percent had negotiated discounts from fees. The average discount in 1991 was 20 percent.[17]

These data suffer from the same limitations that the hospital payment data do. The aforementioned HIAA data on commercial insurers, however, also indicated that PPOs and HMOs do not pay physician billed charges. These data are arrayed in figure 3–5. HMOs and PPOs tend to differ in the way they pay physicians. HMOs are

---

Physician Services," *Socioeconomic Characteristics of Medical Practice 1992* (Chicago, Ill.: American Medical Association, 1992), pp. 11–15.

17. Although the AMA does not provide information on the extent to which physicians have negotiated price reductions for HMOs, PPOs, or other managed-care plans, it does report that such affiliations are both common and of economic significance to physicians. It reports that 70 percent of physicians had a contract with an alternative delivery system (an HMO, Independent Practice Association [IPA], or PPO), and of those who did, these contracts represented 32 percent of their revenue, on average. See Kurt D. Gillis and David W. Emmons, "Physician Involvement with Alternative Delivery Systems," *Socioeconomic Characteristics of Medical Practice 1993* (Chicago, Ill.: American Medical Association, 1993), pp. 15–19.

FIGURE 3–5
PRINCIPAL METHODS OF PAYING PHYSICIANS: COMMERCIAL
INSURER–SPONSORED HMOS AND PPOS, 1990

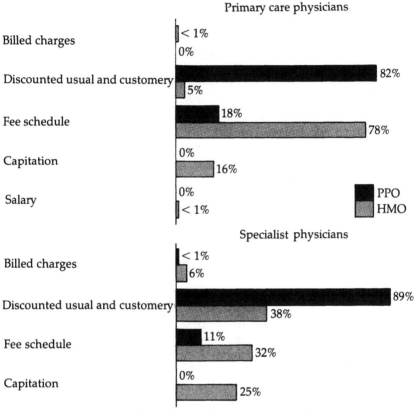

Percentage of insurers (weighted by total premium)

SOURCE: Elizabeth W. Hoy, Richard E. Curtis, and Thomas Rice, "Change and Growth in Managed Care," *Health Affairs*, vol. 10, no. 4 (Winter 1991), pp. 28–29.

reported to place greater reliance than PPOs on fee schedules and capitation arrangements.

Trends in Hospital List Prices and Transaction Prices

As we have seen, hospitals set list prices and typically negotiate and accept lower prices from virtually all payers. It is reported to be com-

31

mon for a hospital to set relatively high list prices and then use these prices as a basis for negotiation. If that is true, this practice has two implications. First, it suggests that measures of hospital inflation based upon list prices are overstatements. Second, it suggests that the spread between list and transaction prices will grow as hospitals try to compete on a price basis by offering big discounts from high list prices. Of course, one would expect the gap between list and transaction prices to expand only until buyers routinely understand how the game is played.

A study by David Dranove and colleagues offers a test of these implications.[18] The Bureau of Labor Statistics has until recently used hospital list prices in its calculation of the hospital component of the Consumer Price Index. The Dranove team was able to calculate a price index based upon California hospital list prices and transaction prices over the period 1984 through 1988. The results are shown in figure 3–6. List prices always increased more rapidly than transaction prices. Over the 1985 to 1987 period list prices increased at an annualized 10.9 percent while transaction prices increased by only 4.8 percent. In addition, since 1985 the difference in the rates of increase between list and transaction prices has expanded.

California is certainly not a typical state. A large portion of its population is enrolled in PPOs and HMOs, and there is evidence that these organizations negotiate prices with hospitals. There is also evidence that changes in the insurance laws in California since 1983 have allowed providers to offer price concessions to different payers.

Work by the Health Care Financing Administration corroborates the Dranove study using national data.[19] It compares trends in hospital list prices as measured by the Consumer Price Index–Hospital Component with patient revenue received per unit of output derived from American Hospital Association Annual Survey data. The results are presented in figure 3–7. Transaction prices rose more slowly than

18. David Dranove, Mark Shanley, and William D. White, "How Fast Are Hospital Prices Really Rising?" *Medical Care*, vol. 29, no. 8 (August 1991), pp. 690–96.

19. Charles R. Fisher, "Trends in Total Hospital Financial Performance under the Prospective Payment System," *Health Care Financing Review*, vol. 13, no. 1 (Spring 1992), pp. 1–16. The Dranove and HCFA trends are also supported by the MEDSTAT analysis of hospital charges on the twenty-five top DRGs in its database of large employers. It found that the rates of increase in its charge index were always below that of the CPI–hospital component since 1989, and by the end of 1991 had an annual rate of increase of 3.1 percent. This was below the economywide general inflation rate of 1991. See *The MEDSTAT Report*, pp. 6–7.

FIGURE 3–6
CALIFORNIA HOSPITAL LIST PRICES AND TRANSACTION PRICES, 1984–1988

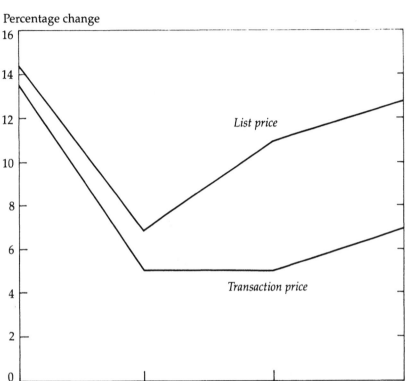

SOURCE: David Dranove, Mark Shanley, and William D. White, "How Fast Are Hospital Prices Really Rising?" *Medical Care*, vol. 29, no. 8 (August 1991), pp. 690–96.

list prices in every year but one during the 1978–1989 period. Further, during the last half of the 1980s the difference in the rates of increase widened. There are a variety of possible explanations for the growing gap. Part of the explanation lies with the implementation of the Medicare prospective payment system (PPS). Part of it may also be explained by the growth of managed care and price competition. We visit issues of hospital price competition in chapter 6.

Summary

The preceding discussion had three main points. First, it demonstrated that hospitals commonly charge different payers different

FIGURE 3-7
HCFA ANALYSIS OF HOSPITAL LIST AND TRANSACTION PRICES, 1978–1989

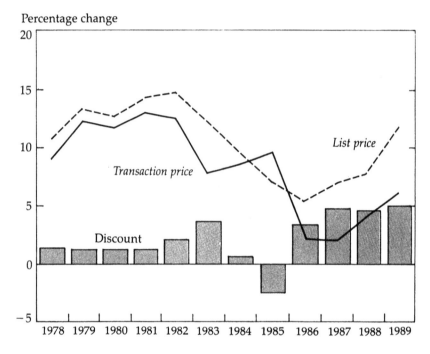

SOURCE: Charles R. Fisher, "Trends in Total Hospital Financial Performance under the Prospective Payment System," *Health Care Financing Review*, vol. 13, no. 1 (Spring 1992), pp. 1–16.

prices for health care services. This practice can be viewed as static cost shifting or as price discrimination, although we have not yet established that the price differences are not justified by cost differences. These data provide no evidence, one way or the other, on dynamic cost shifting, however. Second, the chapter showed that private insurers do not uniformly pay full billed charges. More important, it showed that many private insurers have negotiated pricing schemes that result in payments that are much lower than billed charges. Third, the trends in list and actual prices suggest that many payers may have been successful in their attempts to reduce the rate of increase in hospital prices.

4
The Cost Side of Cost Shifting

Differences in costs may be one reason that hospitals and other providers charge different prices to different categories of payers. We are not surprised to see that oranges are cheaper at a stand alongside the grove than in a supermarket 600 miles away, which must charge for transportation and storage costs. Similarly, one explanation for differences in hospital prices is that patients cost different amounts to treat. In this chapter we examine the cost issues.

We begin by reproducing the cost-shifting paradigm. We then review the research literature on the question of whether different categories of patients are differentially costly to care for. If Medicaid patients are less costly to treat, for example, their lower price is cost-justified and nothing is there to shift. A number of studies purport to address this issue, but I have found only two that do so while controlling for patient and hospital characteristics. They are largely in agreement in their findings. First, when compared on an average-cost-per-day basis, all categories of patients had the same costs. Second, Medicare patients have higher costs and uninsured patients lower costs than privately insured patients when compared on an average-cost-per-admission basis. The differences appear to stem from longer lengths of stay for Medicare patients and shorter stays for the uninsured. Third, although Medicaid patients appear to have higher costs, these are attributable to differences in the costs of the hospitals they use. When these hospital characteristics are accounted for, Medicaid patients are no more costly than privately insured patients. Thus, except for the uninsured group, there is no systematic average cost difference that justifies the differences in prices.

We then return to the pricing theory developed in chapter 2 and add the average cost story as presented by those who believe that cost shifting does occur. The facts are consistent with a profit-maximizing view of hospitals in which all payers cover their marginal costs but some make greater contributions to fixed costs than do others. This distinction is important because it offers an explanation other than goodness-of-heart to explain why many hospitals continue to provide care to Medicare and Medicaid patients even when they appear to be

FIGURE 4-1
PROTOTYPICAL MODEL OF COST SHIFTING

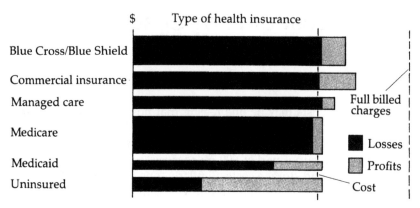

SOURCE: Donald Moran and John Sheils, *Employee Cost-Shifting Expenditures*, Washington, D.C.: Lewin/ICF (September 12, 1991), p. 3.

losing money. The answer is that they may not be losing money. It also calls into question the claim that those who pay the low prices do not make their "fair share" contribution to the fixed costs of running the hospital.

The Cost Shifting Claims

Lewin/ICF make the cleanest presentation of the cost shifting story.[1] Their argument is presented in figure 4-1. Hospitals set full billed charges. Most payers pay something less than this, as is indicated by the vertical bars, which are all below the line showing full billed charges. The cost of treating patients is depicted as the dark horizontal line. Private insurers are shown as paying more than costs. The profit from them is the shaded boxes at the top of their bars. Government payers and the uninsured are said to pay less than the cost of care. The hatched areas reflect the losses the hospital incurs by treating these patients. Hospitals are said to "make up" these losses with the profits they receive from the private payers.

The ratio of hospital payments to cost by payer category is offered

---

1. Donald Moran and John Sheils, *Employer Cost-Shifting Expenditures*, final report of Lewin/ICF to the National Association of Manufacturers (Washington, D.C., September 12, 1991).

TABLE 4-1
ESTIMATES OF RATIO OF HOSPITAL TRANSACTION PRICES TO COSTS
(percentage)

	1989	1990	1992
Private insurance	125.5	127.6	138.3
Medicare	80.5	89.6	85.1
Medicaid	78.5	80.1	78.3
Other government	96.3	106.4	94.4
Uninsured	56.4	21.0	55.3

SOURCE: 1989 and 1992 figures are from Allen Dobson and James Roney, *Cost-Shifting: A Self Limiting Process* (Washington, D.C.: Lewin-ICF, April 1992), Appendix 1. 1990 data are from Prospective Payment Assessment Commission, *Optional Hospital Payment Rates*, Congressional Report C-92-03 (Washington, D.C.: March 1993), p. 29.

as evidence of dynamic cost shifting. Estimates of these ratios for the years 1989 through 1991 are shown in table 4-1. Privately insured patients are seen to pay something between 125 percent and nearly 140 percent of cost. Medicare pays 80 percent to 90 percent of cost; Medicaid approximately 80 percent. The values for the uninsured vary significantly by source and appear to reflect differences in the treatment of direct government subsidies. Generally speaking, private ratios have increased and government ratios have fallen. All this is consistent with the graphic in figure 4-1.

Two important questions emerge from this analysis. First, are the costs of treating different categories of patients actually the same as depicted in figure 4-1 and assumed in the analysis underlying table 4-1. Are Medicaid patients, for example, as costly as privately insured patients? If they are not, the apparent losses from Medicaid are overstated and may not even be losses at all.

Second, even if the average costs are equal, are the marginal costs of care less than average costs? If they are, then differential pricing still does not result in a shifting of costs. One can easily show that a profit-maximizing hospital would rationally price care for one or more categories of patients below average costs as long as that price covers marginal costs—and particularly if it makes some contribution to fixed costs. In the simple textbook model, a firm selling at one price would go out of business if it did not cover all its costs in the long run. When price discrimination is possible, however, pricing one or more markets below average costs can be a successful long-run strategy.

Differential Costs of Care

A number of studies have examined the issue of differential costs across categories of payers. Focusing on Medicaid costs, Glenn Melnick and Joyce Mann provide an excellent review of most of these studies. They summarize this literature as providing mixed results: "In general they provide some evidence that Medicaid patients stay longer than privately insured patients and have a higher average cost per case. Studies conducted using hospital level data show that higher proportions of Medicaid patients increase average hospital cost per admission."[2] Many of the studies are fifteen or twenty years old, however, and several are based on a single hospital. Others fail to control for the types of cases particular hospitals have (so-called case mix) and for hospital differences. A particularly important issue is the direction of causation. Do Medicaid patients cost more, or do Medicaid patients use hospitals that cost more?

Two carefully designed studies overcome many of these problems. The first is by Frank Sloan and Ned Becker.[3] They use 1979 American Hospital Association data from some 1,400 hospitals. They performed a regression analysis of total hospital costs per day and per admission, adjusting for outpatient services. The regression analysis controlled for hospital characteristics (ownership, teaching status, size, services, and capital stock) and market characteristics (income, population density, specialty and generalist physician densities, wage rates, and region). In addition, the study was the first to control for differences in hospital case mix. Of interest to us, the models included variables for the proportion of hospital charges accounted for by six categories of patients and also a measure of the discounts that the hospital provided. Hospital discounts were considered to be endogenous, which means that costs and discounts are determined simultaneously. If one fails to account for this, the coefficients in the cost regressions will be biased and the results misleading.

Sloan and Becker found that, after controlling for other factors, patients had equal costs *per day*, regardless of payer category. Average costs *per admission* were a different story. Hospitals with larger proportions of both Medicare and Medicaid patients had higher costs per

---

2. Glenn A. Melnick and Joyce M. Mann, "Are Medicaid Patients More Expensive? A Review and Analysis," *Medical Care Review*, vol. 46, no. 3 (Fall 1989), pp. 229–53.

3. Frank A. Sloan and Edmund R. Becker, "Cross-Subsidies and Payment for Hospital Care," *Journal of Health Politics, Policy and Law*, vol. 8, no. 4 (Winter 1984), pp. 660–85.

admission. Since costs per day were equal, the greater costliness of these patients was attributable to longer lengths of stay.

Of particular importance, Sloan and Becker concluded that apparent differences in costs across payers had more to do with the choice of hospital used than with the characteristics of the patients. Simply finding differences in costs across payers in a group of hospitals is no evidence that their costs of treatment are actually different.

There are problems with this study. The most important is that the data predate the Medicare PPS, the growth of HMOs and PPOs, and the reduced payment levels implemented by Medicaid. Further, the payer proportions and hospital costs are also likely to be endogenous.

Melnick and Mann overcome many of these problems.[4] They examined 1982 patient data from the state of New Jersey. Although the data are old, they do reflect the incentives that are present in a DRG-type system because at that time New Jersey was in the third year of its all-payer DRG demonstration. The all-payer nature of the demonstration also means that costs reported by hospitals are not influenced by the different reimbursement systems used by the various payers.[5]

They ran patient-level cost and length-of-stay regressions for 236,471 patients from ninety-six of the ninety-eight New Jersey hospitals. This constituted a 20 percent random sample of patients. Costs and length of stay were estimated as a function of the payer category of the patient, the patient's DRG, age, sex, and whether the admission was elective or not. Two alternative sets of hospital and market characteristics were used. The first included an index of hospital input prices, teaching, and location in inner city, urban, suburban, and rural areas. The second set was a series of ninety-five 1–0 variables, one representing each hospital. A variable would take the value 1 if the patient was treated at that hospital. Costs were measured as operating costs. Not considered were overhead, capital, and direct teaching costs.

The findings are summarized in table 4–2 and reflect the model in which the set of hospital variables was used. They show that for patients with the same diagnosis, Medicare beneficiaries had costs

---

4. Melnick and Mann, "Are Medicaid Patients More Expensive?"

5. Patricia Danzon has convincingly argued, for example, that Medicare's historical approach of paying hospitals on the basis of allowable costs effectively turned reported hospital costs into the price paid by Medicare. See Patricia Munch Danzon, "Hospital 'Profits': The Effects of Reimbursement Policies," *Journal of Health Economics*, vol. 1, no. 1 (May 1992), pp. 29–52.

TABLE 4–2
AVERAGE HOSPITAL COSTS FOR NON-PRIVATELY INSURED PATIENTS, 1982
(privately insured patients = 100%)

	Cost per Case (%)	Cost per Day (%)
Medicare	128.8	97.0
Medicaid	101.9	97.5
Self-paying (uninsured)	91.4	100.5
Other paying	103.3	98.5

SOURCE: Computed from Glenn A. Melnick and Joyce M. Mann, "Are Medicaid Patients More Expensive? A Review and Analysis," *Medical Care Review*, vol. 46, no. 3 (Fall 1989), pp. 229–53.

per case that were nearly 29 percent higher. Medicaid cases were nearly 2 percent more costly. Self-paying (uninsured) patients, had average costs that were nearly 9 percent lower than those of privately insured patients. These differences were almost entirely attributable to differences in length of stay. Costs per day were generally two to three percentage points lower for Medicare and Medicaid patients. Like Sloan and Becker, Melnick and Mann found that the apparently higher costs for all categories of non-privately insured patients largely disappeared when one controlled for the hospitals used by these patients. This was particularly true for Medicaid patients.

In summary, the empirical literature on average cost differences across payer categories suggests that the assumption of equal costs per admission across payer categories is largely justified for all but Medicare beneficiaries and the uninsured. The former have higher costs and the latter lower costs. These differences are largely attributable to differences in length of stay.

However, these studies do not reflect the remarkable changes that have occurred in the hospital and insurance markets in the past decade. As a result of PPS Medicare, lengths of stay are shorter.[6] Utilization review has shortened the lengths of stay of privately insured patients.[7] The growth of HMOs, PPOs, and managed care is

6. Frank A. Sloan, Michael A. Morrisey, and Joseph Valvona, "Effects of the Medicare Prospective Payment System on Hospital Cost Containment: An Early Assessment," *Milbank Quarterly*, vol. 66, no. 2 (1988), pp. 191–220.

7. Richard M. Scheffler, Sean D. Sullivan, and T. H. Ko, "The Impact of Blue Cross and Blue Shield Plan Utilization Management Programs, 1980–1988," *Inquiry*, vol. 28, no. 3 (Fall 1991), pp. 263–75. Thomas M. Wickizer, "The Effect of Utilization Review on Hospital Use and Expenditures: A Review of the Literature and An Update on Recent Findings," *Medical Care Review*, vol. 47, no. 3 (1990), pp. 327–63.

FIGURE 4–2
HOSPITAL PRICING RECONSIDERED

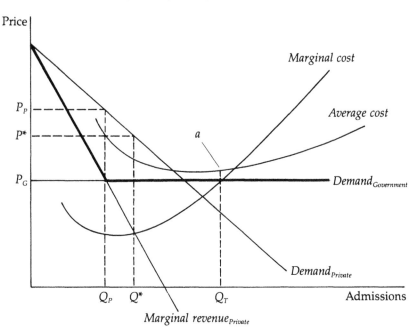

SOURCE: Author.

changing the market in which hospitals operate. We do not really know the relative costliness of patients by payer class in today's environment.

Theory Again

The theory that we presented in chapter 2 focused on marginal revenue and marginal costs. We gave no attention to issues of average costs. We do so now in the context of the cost-shifting model described by figure 4–1 in which all payer categories are assumed to have equal average costs.

The analysis begins with the same profit-maximizing assumptions used in chapter 2. Figure 4–2 replicates our earlier model of a hospital with two categories of payers: government and private. The profit-maximizing solution was to allocate hospital volume in accordance with marginal revenue in the two markets and with marginal costs. This resulted in a governmentally determined price of P_G and a private price of P_P.

The question is whether our rational profit- and utility-maximizing hospital models are consistent with the stylized facts presented by the cost-shifting story.[8] The answer from figure 4–2 is that, yes, they are. The facts are that privately insured payers pay more than costs and government payers pay less. Costs are understood to be facilitywide average costs, which are necessarily determined at the total output of the hospital. This is the point "a" on the average cost curve corresponding to Q_T. Notice that average costs exceed the price the government pays at this point. Notice too, that the private price exceeds this average cost.

But the profit-maximizing hospital is not losing money on government patients. The *marginal* cost curve reflects the additional costs of providing care. In this instance government-sponsored patients generate enough money to cover the marginal costs of treating them and also make a contribution to the fixed costs of the hospital.

In fact, this is a stable, long-run solution in our model. In contrast, in the typical textbook example in which a monopolist sells in a single market *at a single price*, that price would have to exceed average cost at the chosen level of output. Otherwise the firm would not be able to remain in the market.[9] That case is different from ours because of multiple buyers. These buyers have different degrees of price sensitivity, and they pay different prices as a result. In this case, price discrimination, in which some payers pay less than average costs, can cover long-run costs and generate more revenue than any other feasible solution.

To see this, consider what would happen if the hospital decided to stop providing care to government-sponsored patients. It would staff fewer beds and shift some capacity to the private market. This extra capacity could only be sold at a lower price. As drawn in figure 4–2 this implies selling Q^* private admissions at price P^*. This solution maximizes the single-market profit. However, the hospital necessarily makes less profit than in the two-market case. It gives up all of

8. Recall that the profit-maximizing and utility-maximizing hospital models yield the same implications for hospital pricing behavior in most instances. In most instances the only difference is how the hospital spends its profit or surplus. Things are different only when the utility-maximizing hospital favors paying patients by charging them less than it could. See chapter 2.

9. In fact, when a monopolist's price does not exceed average cost at the point where marginal revenue and marginal cost are equal, it is a case of *natural* monopoly. Here a public utility is often created and price is set equal to average cost.

the government cases, each of which generated revenue greater than marginal costs, and it replaces some of the government volume with private patients who generate less marginal revenue than did the government patients. Depending on the extent of the fixed costs, it is even possible to construct a case in which the absence of government patients causes the hospital to close. In such a case the partial contribution to fixed costs made by the government payers, together with the high price to the private payers, would have been just enough to make it worthwhile for the hospital to continue operations. When the hospital stopped providing services to the government patients it was no longer able to cover long-run costs.

Now consider an alternative case, in which the payment from the government-sponsored patient is less than the marginal cost of providing service. This too would be consistent with the stylized facts of cost shifting because it would again show the payment by government payers to be less than the average costs and payments from private payers to be more than the average. In this case, however, government payers are not covering the extra costs of care, much less making a contribution to fixed costs. The profit-maximizing hospital (and the one that does not value government patients per se) will reduce the amount of care it provides to them. If the payment level is sufficiently low, it will stop providing care in the government market entirely. This outcome appears unrealistic in the Medicare hospital market, but only because the payment level is not yet too low. Many hospitals have reduced the amount of Medicaid care they provide, and others have dropped out of the Medicaid program.[10]

It is important to note that this view of hospital costs is consistent with many of the statements of those who assert that cost shifting occurs. The government payers are not covering the *full costs* of their patients. But the perspective one takes on this observation depends upon where one stands. Yes, the government payers are not paying the full costs; however, if the private payers suddenly ceased to exist, the hospital would continue to provide care to government patients and would seek to provide care to more of them. It would do so until it could get out of its long-term contracts.

From another perspective, if the hospital were to stop providing care to government patients, it would lower its price to private patients. But this would have nothing to do with private patients' no longer bearing some of the costs of government payers. The government did pay the marginal costs of treating its patients. If the govern-

10. John Holahan, "The Impact of Alternative Hospital Payment Systems on Medicaid Costs," *Inquiry*, vol. 25, no. 4 (Winter 1988), pp. 517–32.

ment payer disappeared, the fixed costs would still be there and would still have to be paid by the private payers in the long run if the hospital were to continue operating. It would lower its prices, however, to attract more private patients.

Summary

This chapter accomplished two objectives. The first objective was to determine whether differences in hospital prices are justified by differences in costs. First, we reviewed the empirical literature on differences in average costs across different categories of payers. The research literature that controls for case mix and hospital characteristics is remarkably sparse, but it is consistent in three findings: (1) Hospital costs per day are essentially the same for all categories of payers. (2) Hospital costs per admission are somewhat higher for Medicare patients and somewhat lower for uninsured patients than they are for privately insured patients. These cost differences are the result of differences in length of stay. (3) A large component of the apparent differences in the costs of care for different categories of patients can be attributed to the disproportionate differences in the hospitals used. Medicaid patients, for example, are disproportionately cared for in higher-cost teaching hospitals. It is the difference in hospitals used, much more than the difference in patients treated, that explains differences in costs.

On the basis of this literature we can conclude that the observed differences in hospital prices are not cost-justified. The pattern of real-world hospital prices reflects price discrimination or static cost shifting, not cost differences.

The second objective was to consider hospital prices in the context of both average and marginal costs. We have seen that even a profit-maximizing hospital can rationally charge prices below average cost to one (or more) category of payers and above average costs to other classes. However, these differences need *not* imply that one set of payers subsidizes the other. We demonstrated that as long as each group covers the marginal cost of its services, no group is subsidizing any other.

This result highlights an important interpretation of the claims about cost shifting. It is commonly said that one group of patients is not paying its fair share of costs. This claim does not imply that those patients are being subsidized. In the context of marginal costs that are less than average costs, it implies that some patient classes are not making a full contribution to the fixed costs of the hospital. This is a classic economic issue. The allocation of fixed costs is, by definition, arbitrary. The market assigns these costs to the payers that are the least price sensitive. Regulators often do it differently.

Two important insights may be drawn from this interpretation of the "fair share" argument. First, it is now clear what hospital administrators and selected insurers mean by this argument. It is not a subsidy issue; it is an allocation of fixed costs argument. Second, it is also clear that hospitals are not necessarily losing money by using this strategy. Indeed, they can be profitable in the short and the long run as long as the group paying the high prices is sufficiently price insensitive.

5
Evidence of Dynamic Cost Shifting

In this chapter we go to the heart of the cost-shifting story. We examine the empirical evidence on whether hospitals have been able to successfully raise prices to some categories of payers when the prices paid by others fall or when the "need to cost shift" increases. Four published papers address the question with respect to hospitals. The results are mixed. Two studies find evidence of substantial dynamic cost shifting. Two others conclude that there is no meaningful dynamic cost shifting in the hospital industry. Three of the four studies are from the late 1970s and early 1980s. Only one study—which does not find evidence of cost shifting—covers the post-PPS period.

We corroborate this direct evidence with analyses of the effects of Medicaid price reductions on the volume of Medicaid services provided by hospitals, and the effects of PPO-negotiated price reductions on the provision of uncompensated care. These serve as indirect evidence. In either instance a casual interpretation of the cost-shifting argument would lead one to expect that, in the face of Medicaid and PPO price reductions, charges to other payers would be increased and services to Medicaid and PPO patients would be unaffected. In both instances, though, the studies say that the volume of uninsured and Medicaid-insured care fell dramatically. Finally, we examine the one study that looks for dynamic cost shifting in the physician market. It finds evidence of dynamic cost shifting but is better viewed as a study in physician-induced demand rather than cost shifting.

Direct Hospital Evidence

Dynamic cost shifting exists when a price cut by one payer, typically a government payer such as Medicaid or Medicare, results in higher prices paid by others, typically private insurers. The strongest evidence of such cost shifting is provided by David Dranove.[1] He examined price cuts by the Medicaid program of Illinois over the period 1981 to 1983. During that time the program reduced its per diem

---

1. Dranove, "Pricing by Non-Profit Institutions."

payments to hospitals, introduced limitations on reimbursable admissions, and placed ceilings on reimbursable inpatient days. Accounting profits in 1983 from Medicare and Medicaid sources were $1.9 million higher than they were in 1981 for the average hospital in his sample. These accounting profits were defined as the difference between actual government (that is, Medicare and Medicaid) payments and expenditures.[2]

Dranove tests for the size of dynamic cost shifting by running a regression in which the change in the private patient price is a function of the change in these government profits, controlling for the change in costs per admission and the change in the number of beds set up and staffed in the hospital's metropolitan area. This latter variable is intended to control for changes in the competitive nature of the hospital's environment. The private price is measured as hospital inpatient revenues actually received, minus Medicare and Medicaid revenues, divided by non-Medicare and non-Medicaid admissions. The data for the analysis come from the 79 (of 280) Illinois hospitals that were nonprofit, located in a metropolitan area, and provided the requisite data in both years on the American Hospital Association's Annual Survey of Hospitals.

This analytic approach has two particular strengths. First, the focus on Illinois limits cross-sectional demand or supply shocks, which would tend to bias the findings against a cost-shifting result. Second, the use of change variables allows each hospital to serve as its own control. Note, though, that the data predate the Medicare prospective payment system and the growth in PPOs. Also, the hospitals are not representative of Illinois hospitals, much less of hospitals nationwide. The study underrepresents those hospitals that have a disproportionate share of government-sponsored patients. These factors limit the generalizability of the results, but do not affect the test of dynamic cost shifting.

Dranove finds that a $1,000 reduction in government profits led to a fifteen-cent increase in the price per private admission. With an alternative specification Dranove found that a one-dollar reduction in government profits *per private admission* led to a fifty-one-cent increase in the price per private admission. Given the $1.88 million reduction in government accounting profits and the 4,766 private admissions, this implies that the typical hospital in the sample raised its price per private admission by $201.

---

2. As we noted in chapter 4, there is no easy method of determining the costs attributable to a particular class of patients. Dranove assumes that all patients are equally costly. Further, he was unable to separate Medicare and Medicaid patients.

This analysis provides the strongest evidence of dynamic cost shifting. It is important to note, however, that even this evidence does not imply that the hospital that raises its prices to privately insured patients totally recovers the revenue lost from Medicaid. Dranove found that a one-dollar decrease in hospital profits from government sources per private admission led to a fifty-one-cent increase in the price per private admission. Thus, about one-half of the revenue loss was recovered.

There is some reason to speculate, however, that the estimates may overstate the actual effect of cost shifting. Based upon the sample means of the number of private admissions and the inflation-adjusted private prices in 1981 and 1983, the implied private price elasticity of demand was − .73. That is, a 10 percent increase in the private price reduced private admissions at the typical hospital in the sample by just over 7 percent. This unusually large hospital-specific price response in a period when hospitals were alleged to not be competing on a price basis suggests that other factors may have biased the cost-shifting estimate.

Frank Sloan and Ned Becker were the first to examine the cost-shifting hypothesis with multivariate techniques.[3] They examined the effect of hospital discounts from billed charges given to Medicare, Medicaid, Blue Cross, and some commercial payers on the accounting profits received from commercial insurers. This profit was measured as patient revenue received divided by total costs. Accounting profit (both in aggregate and from patient care only) was regressed on the discount; the proportion of revenues from different payers; hospital characteristics including ownership, teaching, bed size, outpatient care, available services, and hospital capital; and market and region characteristics. The authors appreciate that the private profit and the size of the discount are simultaneously determined, so they estimated a two-equation model. Sloan and Becker used data from the 1979 AHA Reimbursement Survey of over 1,400 nonprofit U.S. community hospitals, and their analysis is purely cross-sectional in nature.

They found that larger discounts to Medicare, Medicaid, Blue Cross, and others were associated with *lower*, not higher, total profits. As the authors write: "Put differently, the question here is whether hospitals are able to shift costs from one payer to another and fully recover their costs. We find they cannot."[4] The emphasis here is on *fully* recovering costs. Sloan and Becker did find that the hospitals studied charged higher private prices but also offered private payers

---

3. Sloan and Becker, "Cross-Subsidies and Payment for Hospital Care."
4. Ibid., p. 677.

larger discounts. The average discount to noncommercial payers was approximately 15.5 percent. Commercial payers were charged 4–5 percent more per admission, on average. Given the relative shares of admissions, the implication is that up to 90 percent of the discounts were made up for by commercial payers.

There are problems with this study, not the least of which is that the data are fourteen years old. In addition, the study is purely cross-sectional in nature. Any market-specific factors that enhance the hospital's market power with local commercial payers will lead to higher private prices. Rather than observing cost shifting per se, the Sloan and Becker study may have picked up simple differences in market power. The Dranove model, with its use of changes across time periods, is less susceptible to this problem.

Stephen Zuckerman also examined the hospital cost-shifting issue; his work is the strongest evidence that dynamic cost shifting is not a significant problem.[5] He builds on work by Jack Hadley and Judy Feder in first measuring the "need to cost shift" and then empirically investigating whether those hospitals with the greatest need at the beginning of the period increased their private prices the most.[6] The need to cost shift is based on the sum of the costs of uncompensated care; the difference between the costs and revenues associated with inpatient care provided to Medicare, Medicaid, and Blue Cross patients; and the difference between nonpatient care expenses and revenues.[7] This index, therefore, allows for discounts to various pay-

5. Stephen Zuckerman, "Commercial Insurers and All-Payer Regulation," *Journal of Health Economics*, vol. 6, no. 2 (September 1987), pp. 165–87.

6. Jack Hadley and Judy Feder, "Hospital Cost Shifting and Care for the Uninsured," *Health Affairs*, vol. 4, no. 3 (Fall 1985), pp. 67–80. Hadley and Feder develop the index and relate it to private markups. They found that the half of their sample with the greatest need to cost shift would have had to raise prices by 37 percent. In fact, these hospitals raised prices by less than 1 percent. In contrast, the half of the sample with less need should have reduced prices by nearly 14 percent if the literal view of cost shifting were true. Instead, they increased prices by nearly 2.3 percent. The Hadley-Feder analysis suffers because it did not control for other factors.

7. The need to cost shift is defined as: $100 \times \{1 + [(FN/DAY)/COST]\}$. FN is the financial need of the hospital as defined in the text. DAY is the number of commercial patient days and COST is average cost per inpatient day. If a hospital breaks even on its uncompensated care, discounts, and revenues from subsidies and philanthropic sources, the need-to-cost-shift index has the value of 100. A value of 125 would imply that the expected percentage markup of revenues above costs is 25 percent. A surplus would imply that the index was less than 100 and a "markdown" could occur.

ers and the provision of charity care, net of government subsidies, philanthropy, and nonpatient profits.

In his regression model the markup to commercial insurers was defined as the average revenue per commercially insured inpatient day as a percentage of the average cost per day. This was regressed on the need-to-cost-shift variable and variables controlling for region, bed size, teaching status, and market characteristics. The model also included the base year commercial markup, allowing Zuckerman to consider changes in the commercial markup over time. As with the earlier two studies, this one uses data that are now quite old. The analysis is based on data from 204 nonprofit hospitals nationwide that responded to the AHA Medical Care for the Poor Surveys for 1980 and 1982.

Zuckerman used two different specifications of the need-to-cost-shift index. In the simplest, the index is included in the commercial markup equation. It yields only a small and statistically insignificant effect and provides no evidence of dynamic cost shifting.

As an alternative, hospitals were classified as having a low, moderate, or high need to cost shift. This approach yields results generally consistent with Hadley and Feder's.[8] That is, hospitals with a low need to cost shift charged prices to commercial insurers that were more than 11 percentage points higher than hospitals with no need. Those in the middle range had markups more than seventeen percentage points higher. Those with the greatest need had markups not statistically different from those with no need. All this suggests that it is not the "need to cost shift" that leads a hospital to raise its prices to commercially insured patients.

Suppose commercially insured patients (or their insurers) have some market power themselves and that higher prices lead them to use less hospital care or to use other hospitals. In this scenario when commercial payers constitute a larger share of a hospital's patient base the hospital is less likely to raise prices. Zuckerman tested this by combining the need-to-cost-shift index with the share of hospital days paid for by commercial insurers. The results are summarized in figure 5–1. When a hospital had a small share of privately insured patients, say 5 percent, as its need to cost shift increased it raised private prices as shown in the top line in the figure. If this hospital had a need index value of 125 it would have to raise prices to commercial insurers by 25 percent to cover this need. Figure 5–1, based upon the regression coefficients, indicates that it actually was able to raise

---

8. Hadley and Feder, "Hospital Cost Shifting and Care for the Uninsured."

FIGURE 5–1
HOSPITAL PRICE INCREASES RESULTING FROM THE NEED TO COST SHIFT

Private price increase (%)

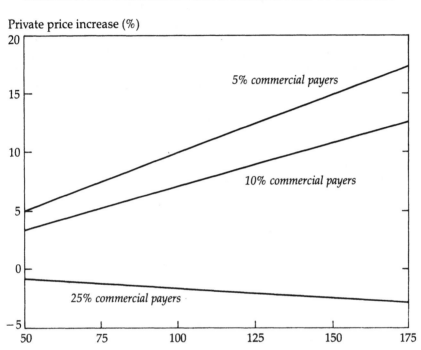

Index of need to cost shift

SOURCE: Stephen Zuckerman, "Commercial Insurers and All-Payer Regulation," *Journal of Health Economics*, vol. 6 (September 1987), pp. 167–87.

its prices only 12.4 percent. In contrast, a hospital with the same need to cost shift and where commercially insured patients accounted for 25 percent of patient days actually *reduced* its commercial prices by 2.1 percent.

One interpretation of this finding is that when commercial insurers constituted a relatively large share of hospital admissions, hospitals feared losing these admissions and did not raise their prices. In fact, the evidence for hospitals in this circumstance is that they *lowered* their prices, just as conventional economic theory predicts. It is also important to note that even those hospitals that did raise prices raised them by only about half as much as the need index suggested they would.

A relevant question is which of these markup paths is the more typical. The answer is that the average share of inpatient days paid

51

by commercial insurers in the Zuckerman sample was 23 percent. The typical hospital appears to be more like the hospital that did not raise prices *as a result* of charity loads and discounts to governmental payers.[9]

The last multivariate analysis of hospital cost shifting comes from Blue Cross data. With the implementation of the Medicare prospective payment system there was concern that lower prices paid by Medicare would lead to dynamic cost shifting to private payers, including Blue Cross. Richard Scheffler and colleagues investigated this issue using quarterly Blue Cross plan data from sixty-one plans during the 1980–1986 period.[10] They regressed Blue Cross inpatient payments per 1,000 subscribers and inflation-adjusted payments per admission on a measure of PPS, utilization management programs that had been implemented by Blue Cross, and plan, market, and demographic characteristics.

They found that a 10 percent increase in the proportion of PPS-paid Medicare days resulted in a one-tenth of 1 percent reduction in the inflation-adjusted inpatient expenditures per 1,000 Blue Cross subscribers. This translates into a 1986 Blue Cross savings of $506.8 million. The savings were largely the result of reduced admissions, which presumably resulted from a spillover of practice style changes from Medicare to Blue Cross. A 10 percent increase in Medicare PPS days also did lead to a one-tenth of 1 percent increase in the Blue Cross inflation-adjusted payment per admission. The authors do not attribute this to cost shifting, however. Rather, they see it as an artifact of a PPS-induced longer length of stay. The less sick patients were no longer admitted to the hospital, so the average stay of those actually admitted appeared to rise.[11]

---

9. Other analyses have begun to use measures similar to Zuckerman's "need to cost shift." ProPAC has used 1989 hospital data to compute private payment-to-cost ratios as a function of the need to cost shift. Those with no need (7 percent of hospitals) had payment ratios of 1.30, on average. The 47 percent with a moderate need had ratios of 1.25, and those with the greatest need had payment-to-cost ratios of 1.30. On their face these data do not support the view that higher need led to higher private prices; however, the analysis did not control for other factors. See Prospective Payment Assessment Commission, *Medicare and the American Health Care System*, p. 67.

10. Richard M. Scheffler, James O. Gibbs, and Delores A. Gurnick, *The Impact of Medicare's Prospective Payment System and Private Section Initiatives: Blue Cross Experience, 1980–1985*, report to HCFA (Chicago: Blue Cross and Blue Shield Association, 1988).

11. To my knowledge there is only one other multivariate analysis of hospital cost shifting. This one was conducted by Frank Sloan and me. See Michael

Indirect Evidence on Dynamic Cost Shifting

There are two sets of analyses that might be called indirect tests of the dynamic cost-shifting hypotheses. These tests derive from the casual view that hospitals choose to provide care to the indigent and to government-sponsored patients. A direct test would look at the effect of government price reductions or the increase in charity care on the prices charged to private patients. An indirect test would look at the effect of Medicaid price cuts on the provision of care to Medicaid-eligible patients and the effects of various cuts by public and private payers on the provision of charity care by hospitals. These tests are not pure. Under a George Bailey–type regime, in which a hospital spends profits on charity care and other like services, such cuts necessarily require the hospital to cut back on care. The hospital with unexploited market power would be expected to optimize across all its objectives, raising prices to favored payers and reducing care to Medicaid patients, for example. Current rhetoric, however, would lead us to believe that hospitals would simply raise prices to some patients and maintain care to the poor or to Medicaid-eligible patients. Thus, these indirect tests are instructive.

John Holahan provides a careful look at the effects of Medicaid payment systems on use of hospital services by Medicaid patients.[12] Since 1982 a number of state Medicaid programs have adopted state rate-setting systems, prospective payment systems, and selective contracting arrangements for the payment of hospitals. Holahan uses American Hospital Association special topics survey data from 1980, 1982, and 1984 to examine the effects of these program changes on

---

A. Morrisey and Frank Sloan, "Hospital Cost Shifting and the Medicare Prospective Payment System," final report to the Health Insurance Association of America, Washington, D.C., 1989. The study uses AHA annual survey data from the period 1980–1987. We found that, as a result of PPS, inflation-adjusted private hospital prices fell by a cumulative 7.0 percent over the four years of the Medicare PPS phase-in. Hospitals with higher Medicaid and self-paying or uninsured patient loads were no more likely to raise prices than other hospitals. We also argued, however, that hospitals in more competitive markets should be less able to cost shift. In this view, we thought rural hospitals should be better able to cost shift than their urban cousins. In contrast, we found that metropolitan hospitals raised their prices to private payers by 18.1 percent during the phase-in, while rural hospitals reduced their prices to these payers by more than 14 percent. These results suggest some problem in the empirical specification of the model. As a consequence, I do not rely on these findings in this review.

12. Holahan, "The Impact of Alternative Hospital Payment Systems."

Medicaid admissions and length of stay. His multivariate regression models control for hospital characteristics such as size, case mix, occupancy, ownership, teaching status, and market and policy variables such as community size, HMO penetration, Medicare payment, and a measure of Medicaid-eligible patients.

The regression results showed that state rate-setting programs reduced Medicaid admissions by about 9 percent, on average. The California selective contracting program cut admissions by 14 percent. Lengths of stay typically increased, presumably as a result of a shift toward admitting only the most seriously ill patients. Holahan concludes: "In summary, rate-setting systems with lower rates for Medicaid patients clearly reduced admissions, with the effect concentrated in private low-Medicaid-volume hospitals. Medicaid admissions also fell in California under selective contracting, although this effect cannot be attributed solely, if at all, to selective contracting. Medicaid-only prospective payment systems also may have resulted in lower levels of Medicaid admissions, particularly among private hospitals."[13] This evidence suggests that instead of continuing to see the same volume of Medicaid patients in the face of Medicaid payment cuts (and raising prices to other payers), hospitals cut back on the volume of Medicaid patients.

There has been considerable research conducted on hospitals' provision of care to the uninsured. Most of these studies have focused on which categories of hospitals provide more or less care. It is well known, for example, that the presence of a public hospital reduces the quantity of charity care provided by local private hospitals.[14]

---

13. Ibid., p. 528. The uncertainty resulting from the California experience derived from an inability to separate the Medicaid selective contracting initiatives from the more general expanded use of price contracting throughout the state. See chapter 6 for a discussion of the California experience.

14. See Richard G. Frank and David S. Salkever, "The Supply of Charity Services by Nonprofit Hospitals: Motives and Market Structure," *Rand Journal of Economics*, vol. 22, no. 3 (Autumn 1991), pp. 430–45; and Sloan et al., "Hospital Care for the 'Self-Pay' Patient." This behavior is not inconsistent with a hospital's desire to see care provided to the uninsured. The problem is the classic one of the provision of "public goods," goods which once provided all benefit. In this case the private hospitals "feel better" when the indigent receive care, regardless of which hospital actually provides the care. An interesting analysis would examine whether the presence of a public hospital providing these services leads to lower prices for private patients at private hospitals. The conventional theories would suggest that no change in prices would occur. The dynamic cost-shifting theory would hypothesize that private prices would be reduced.

There also have been attempts to examine the effects of the Medicare PPS on hospital provision of indigent care. Most of the studies available to date have focused on the early years of the PPS and found little impact, perhaps because the program was not particularly restrictive in its early years.[15]

Jonathan Gruber provides a recent analysis of the effects of private sector price negotiations on the provision of charity care by hospitals.[16] He analyzes 1984–1988 California hospital data. In 1983 California enacted legislation allowing and encouraging providers to enter into contracts with insurers that did not require all insurers to pay the same price. Gruber argues that this action should lead to lower profits and less money to spend on the uninsured. He compares the volume of uncompensated care in 1988 and 1984 as a function of the hospital average private discount; the Medicare PPS; hospital characteristics such as teaching, ownership, and size; and market characteristics such as the percentage of the population uninsured in the metropolitan area, income, and the presence of a public hospital. The discount is endogenous in this model, and Gruber dealt with this by estimating a two-stage model.

He found that a one-dollar increase in the discount led to a fifty-three-cent reduction in the amount of uncompensated care provided. In further probing, Gruber suggests that much of this reduction occurred on the ambulatory care side, with relatively little reduction in inpatient care to the uninsured. This conclusion too suggests that hospitals, at least hospitals in California, are not able to raise prices to some payers to offset price reductions to others. Real services adjust.

Evidence from the Physician Market

The empirical literature on physician responses to price changes has focused almost exclusively on the direct effects on volume. The question has been whether physicians would reduce their services in the face of a price cut (as conventional economic theory would suggest) or increase the volume of their services to maintain their income. The latter view has come to be called the *target income hypothesis.* This discussion has become particularly contentious and will not be en-

15. See Sloan et al., "Hospital Care for the 'Self-Pay' Patient," and Steven Sheingold and Thomas Buchberger, "Implications of Medicare's Prospective Payment System for the Provision of Uncompensated Hospital Care," *Inquiry,* vol. 23, no. 4 (Winter 1986), pp. 371–81.

16. Jonathan Gruber, "The Effect of Price Shopping in Medical Markets: Hospital Responses to PPOs in California," National Bureau of Economic Research, working paper 4190 (New York, October 1992).

tered into here.[17] The early literature on the target income hypothesis focused on why physicians did not raise their prices as much as they could have. With the advent of insurer restrictions on physician fees, the analysis has begun to focus on volume adjustments.[18] This focus implies a presumption that physician fees have not been subject to dynamic cost shifting.

There is one recent study that addresses the issue. Marianne Fahs examined the period 1976–1979, during which the United Mine Workers Health and Retirement Fund introduced worker cost sharing, in which UMW members were assessed a $7.50 copayment each time they visited a physician.[19] Fahs examined data from one group practice of fifteen full-time and thirteen part-time physicians and the services they provided for three common diagnoses. The patients seen by this practice were split fairly evenly between UMW members and others. During the period of study the (less generous) health insurance benefits of the other workers were unchanged. Fahs, therefore, compares aggregate fees per episode and average fees per visit per episode before and after the introduction of the copayment provision, controlling for other factors. She finds that after the introduction of the copayment, the UMW beneficiaries were charged total fees per episode that were 12 percent lower and average fees per visit per episode that were 4 percent lower than they were before.[20] More important for our purposes, Fahs also found that the aggregate fees per episode were 17 percent higher and the average fee per visit per episode was 11 percent higher. This finding seems to imply substantial physician cost shifting.

Things are more complex, however. For the UMW beneficiaries Fahs found that aggregate fees were lower as a result of lower utiliza-

---

17. For alternative reviews of the literature, see Roger Feldman and Frank Sloan, "Competition among Physicians Revisited," *Journal of Health Politics, Policy and Law*, vol. 13, no. 2 (Summer 1988), pp. 239–61; and Thomas H. Rice and Roberta J. Labelle, "Do Physicians Induce Demand for Medical Services?" *Journal of Health Politics, Policy and Law*, vol. 14, no. 3 (Fall 1989), pp. 587–601.

18. Thomas G. McGuire and Mark V. Pauly, "Physician Response to Fee Changes with Multiple Payers," *Journal of Health Economics*, vol. 10, no. 4 (December 1991), pp. 385–410.

19. Marianne C. Fahs, "Physician Response to the United Mine Workers' Cost-Sharing Program: The Other Side of the Coin," *Health Services Research*, vol. 27, no. 1 (April 1992), pp. 25–45.

20. These values were obtained by converting the published coefficients to natural log equivalents and applying a correction for the use of dummy variables in a semi-logarithmic regression.

tion—in particular, they spent fewer days in the hospital and used fewer services per visit. This finding suggests that "fees" should actually be interpreted as expenditures. If so, the lower average fee per visit may also reflect lower utilization in an unmeasured dimension. The higher non-UMW "fees" reflect higher utilization, again, principally in the hospital sector. Thus, rather than providing evidence of cost shifting, the Fahs study is better viewed in the context of the literature on physician-induced demand.[21] Physician-induced demand has important policy implications, but they are different from those of cost shifting.[22]

---

21. There are other possible problems as well. The coefficients appear to be too large. The aggregate increase in revenue from the non-UMW patients swamps the revenue loss from the mine workers. If one adopts the income-versus-substitution model of physician behavior advanced by McGuire and Pauly, one should expect relatively large volume adjustments in the non-UMW market when (1) the fee reduction by the UMW is large, and (2) the margin paid by non-UMW patients was much higher than that paid by the UMW patients. See McGuire and Pauly, "Physician Response to Fee Changes," p. 403.

Fahs maintains that the fee cut was large, although this is debatable and depends upon the elasticity of demand of UMW beneficiaries. However, since both the UMW and non-UMW beneficiaries appear to face the same fee schedule in the initial period, the second condition is not satisfied. One possible explanation may be that the non-UMW effect of the UMW action is captured purely as a time-dependent dummy variable. If inflation or other factors are not adequately controlled for over the three-year period of the study, the non-UMW variable would be biased.

22. There is reason to believe that physicians who alter relationships with insurers will pay a price, at least in some markets. The following story concerns a physician group in a relatively large southeastern city and is taken from a favorable brokerage research report on PhyCor, Inc. PhyCor acquires, owns, and operates multispecialty physician group practices.

> PhyCor recently announced that it would take a non-recurring, non-cash pre-tax charge to its 1992 Q3 earnings related to its [X clinic] in [Y city]. The [clinic], acquired in September 1989, was the only multi-specialty physician group in [city] with 55 physicians and on a capitation fee basis. At the time the clinic was acquired . . . the clinic was launching two satellite facilities and moving from an exclusive relationship with PruCare, an HMO, to one with all HMOs and PPOs. In response, PruCare, which represented 70.0% of the [clinic] revenues, forced all enrollees to select new physicians and excluded the satellite clinics from participating in their plan, thereby effectively terminating their relationship with the [clinic]. As part of its transition strategy which includes . . . a reduction in the number of physicians and support personnel, . . .

Summary

This chapter examined the literature on dynamic cost shifting. Only four studies rigorously address the issue in the hospital industry, and unfortunately, three of the studies predate the advent of the Medicare prospective payment system and the growth of managed care in many parts of the United States. As such their application to today's health care markets should not necessarily be relied on.

Taken together, the studies suggest that dynamic cost shifting is either nonexistent or limited in its application. The studies which did not find dynamic cost shifting to be important, found in one case that those hospitals that received a greater proportion of their revenues from private insurers were less likely to shift costs to these payers even when they had larger charity loads and made price concessions to government payers. The study using the more recent data found that Blue Cross actually saved money with the advent of Medicare prospective payment, which created changes in hospital utilization patterns. Although prices per admission rose somewhat, the authors of the study attributed the increase to more complex cases, not to cost shifting.

The studies that have found evidence of dynamic cost shifting in hospitals find that it is a tool of limited effectiveness. That is, while hospitals may have raised prices to private payers to compensate for price cuts by government payers, the increases were not sufficient to fully offset the revenue reductions. In the more rigorous study, private price increases covered half of the public revenue decline. In the other study increases covered 90 percent.

To my knowledge there is only one study that looks at dynamic cost shifting in the physician market. It finds evidence of price increases in one private market that exceed the reductions in the other. Upon careful inspection, this study actually examines differences in volume and is another of a series of studies of physician-induced demand.

Thus, evidence does exist for at least limited dynamic cost shifting, although, it does not stand unchallenged. The nature of hospital and insurance markets has changed dramatically since the time of these studies, however. In the next chapter we focus on the roles played by managed care and hospital competition. The key ingredient

---

Morgan Keegan Research, "PhyCor, Inc." (September 22, 1992), p. 2. Clearly PhyCor did not believe that it could make up for a fee reduction (to zero) resulting from the loss of PruCare by raising prices to other patients. Instead, it fired physicians and support personnel.

in cost shifting, of either the static or the dynamic variety, is market power on the part of hospitals. The recent evidence suggests that hospital competition leads to price reductions and that managed care entities have been able to negotiate price concessions from hospitals.

6
Seeking Lower Prices: Competition in the Hospital Market

One of the key elements in a hospital's ability to shift costs is that it have market power. This chapter examines the evidence on the effects of market power on hospital pricing behavior.

In chapter 5 we saw that the evidence of dynamic cost shifting was mixed at best. On the one hand, the most rigorous study supporting the existence of dynamic cost shifting found that, at least for the one-third of Illinois hospitals studied, hospitals were able to raise their average private prices by fifty-one cents per admission for every one-dollar loss in public profits per admission. On the other hand, analysis of national data found that those hospitals with even a quarter of their hospital days paid for by commercial insurers did not raise prices to these payers even in the face of a strong "need to cost shift." Blue Cross plan data also suggested that as a result of the Medicare prospective payment system Blue Cross saved money; there was no evidence of dynamic cost shifting. The indirect evidence from Medicaid and the uninsured also suggested that dynamic cost shifting can be of only limited value to providers. Hospitals significantly reduced their services to these categories of patients when payment levels were cut. Effective cost shifting would have made this unnecessary.

Perhaps the most striking point in all the work is the age of the data used in the studies. With the exception of the Blue Cross study, all of the analyses relied on data from the late 1970s or very early 1980s.[1] Since that time the Medicare prospective payment system has

---

1. The reason for this is the lack of generally available data on hospital revenues by payer source. The studies to date have relied on special surveys conducted by the American Hospital Association under contract to the researchers undertaking the study. These surveys included an explicit release of these data for research purposes. The AHA Annual Survey of Hospitals, for example, does collect these data but does not allow their use by anyone outside the AHA.

been enacted and phased in. HMOs have grown to cover nearly 20 percent of the population, and PPOs have become an important force in health care organization.

These events suggest that private insurers have become more prudent in their purchase of hospital care. They are likely to be more price sensitive. If that is true, one would expect that even hospitals that at one time were able to cost shift with reckless abandon, would be much less able to do so today.

In this chapter we examine the recent research literature on the nature of hospital competition, the effects of PPOs, and the use of local hospitals by HMOs. These analyses are drawn largely, but not exclusively, from the California experience because of the changes that have taken place in the California health care markets and the availability of hospital data in California. Although the results certainly cannot be generalized to other markets, they do suggest that price shopping, in less dramatic form, may be going on in other health care markets as well.

Hospital Competition as Historically Viewed

Theories of the hospital market generally view the hospital as competing for patients or physicians or both. Typically one might expect hospitals to behave like other providers of complex services, distinguishing themselves on the basis of the bundle of services, quality, and amenities that they offer and the price they charge. It is argued, however, that the hospital market is very different from that of other services. The presence of widespread health insurance allows individual consumers and their physician-agents to be much less concerned about the price of care. They have the incentive to use every service and amenity available as long as the perceived value is greater than the out-of-pocket cost. Intensive use of services, of course, will drive up the price of insurance, but the "prisoner's dilemma" aspect of the problem makes this largely irrelevant.[2] Thus, in competing for physicians and their patients, hospitals put much more emphasis on

---

2. The "prisoner's dilemma" problem is easily seen as one insured individual in competition with everyone else in the insurance pool. If the individual is conservative in the use of medical services and everyone else uses every unit of service that is worth at least the out-of-pocket cost, then premiums will rise by virtually as much as if the individual were not conservative. But if everyone else is conservative in their use of medical care and the individual is not, he gets both stable premiums and lots of medical care. Thus, it is never in the individual's interest to be "medically conservative."

FIGURE 6–1
ADJUSTED AVERAGE COSTS PER HOSPITAL ADMISSION, 1982

Number of neighboring hospitals within fifteen-mile radius

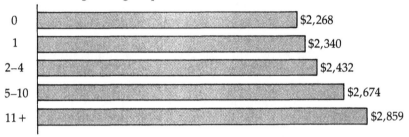

Note: Values are adjusted for hospital characteristics, case mix, population characteristics, and wage rate.
SOURCE: James C. Robinson and Harold S. Luft, "The Impact of Hospital Market Structure on Patient Volume, Average Length of Stay and the Cost of Care" *Journal of Health Economics*, vol. 4, no. 4 (December 1985), pp. 336–56.

the services and amenities they offer than on the prices they charge.[3]

One testable implication of this theory is that the amount of services and costs per admission will be higher in communities with more hospitals because these hospitals must compete for physicians and their patients. A number of researchers have addressed this issue. The work of Jamie Robinson and Hal Luft is perhaps the best.[4] Using data from 1982 they identified the number of hospitals in a fifteen-mile radius of each hospital in the United States. Then, controlling for hospital and population characteristics, case mix, and wage rates, they estimated the effect of the number of potentially competing hospitals on the average cost per admission at each hospital. The results are summarized in figure 6–1. Hospitals with no competitors had an average cost per admission of $2,268; those with eleven or more potential competitors had costs of $2,859. This 26

3. See David Dranove, "The Case for Competitive Reform in Health Care," in *Competitive Approaches to Health Care Reform*, ed. Richard J. Arnould, Robert F. Rich, and William D. White (Washington, D.C.: Urban Institute Press, 1993), pp. 67–87.

4. James C. Robinson and Harold S. Luft, "The Impact of Hospital Market Structure on Patient Volume, Average Length of Stay and the Cost of Care," *Journal of Health Economics*, vol. 4, no. 4 (December 1985), pp. 333–57.

percent higher cost suggests that hospitals have engaged in substantial service and amenity competition.[5]

Hospital Competition in the New Environment

More recent empirical work shows that the nature of the hospital market, at least in some communities, has changed substantially. Glenn Melnick and Jack Zwanziger have examined the effects of changes in California.[6] In 1983 the state of California allowed insurers to selectively contract with providers. It also implemented a selective contracting program that allowed the state Medicaid program to enter into contracts only with hospitals willing to provide inpatient services through a competitive bidding process. These contracts were based, in part, on the prices the hospitals were willing to accept. Melnick and Zwanziger examined the rate of increase in hospital costs in the period before the PPO and selective contracting legislation took effect and after. These are the periods 1980–1982 and 1983–1985. The results are summarized in figure 6–2. In the earlier period hospital costs behaved as the service competition model suggested. Hospitals in communities with more competition had more rapid rates of cost increase than hospitals with fewer competitors, suggesting that the competition had been in the form of services, amenities, and quality enhancements. In the PPO period, however, the hospitals in the

---

5. There has been considerable debate over how one should appropriately define the market area of a hospital. For a review of the issues and the empirical literature, see Michael A. Morrisey, Frank A. Sloan, and Joseph Valvona, "Geographic Markets for Hospital Care," *Law and Contemporary Problems*, vol. 51, no. 2 (September 1989), pp. 165–94. David Dranove and colleagues have argued that the definition of the market used by Robinson and Luft (as well as definitions used by others) has led to the erroneous assumption of greater service rivalry among hospitals in markets with more hospitals. Using California data from 1983, they conclude that there is only minimal support for the so-called medical arms race. Instead they find substantial economies of scope for many services. This means that one hospital service is cheaper to produce *because* the hospital also produces other services. See David Dranove, Mark Shanley, and Carol Simon, "Is Hospital Competition Wasteful?" *Rand Journal of Economics*, vol. 23, no. 2 (Summer 1992), pp. 247–62.

6. Glenn A. Melnick and Jack Zwanziger, "Hospital Behavior under Competition and Cost-Containment Policies," *Journal of the American Medical Association*, vol. 260, no. 18 (November 11, 1988), pp. 2669–75; Jack Zwanziger and Glenn A. Melnick, "The Effects of Hospital Competition and the Medicare PPS Program on Hospital Cost Behavior in California," *Journal of Health Economics*, vol. 7, no. 4 (December 1988), pp. 301–20.

FIGURE 6-2
CHANGE IN CALIFORNIA HOSPITAL COSTS BEFORE AND AFTER PPOs,
1980–1985

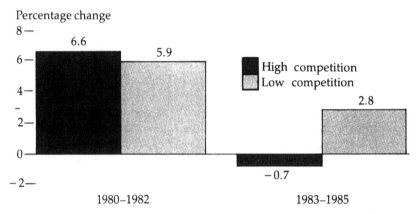

SOURCE: Glenn A. Melnick and Jack Zwanziger, "Hospital Behavior under Competition and Cost-Containment Policies," *Journal of the American Medical Association*, vol. 260, no. 18, (November 11, 1988), pp. 2669–75.

more competitive markets had lower rates of increase. Indeed, their real costs actually dropped slightly. In contrast, the hospitals in *less* competitive markets had more rapid rates of cost increase.[7] Indeed, hospital average costs in more competitive markets have continued to decline throughout the last half of the 1980s, relative to those of hospitals in less competitive markets. In 1980–1982, hospital costs in the more competitive California markets were 12 percent higher than in less competitive markets. Then the selective contracting legislation was enacted. By mid-1988 the costs were equal and in 1989 and 1990 hospitals in more competitive markets had *levels* of average costs below those of less competitive markets.[8] These results suggest that

---

7. In more sophisticated analysis, Zwanziger and Melnick control for hospital output, case mix, input prices, teaching, ownership, and related hospital characteristics, as well as the Medicare PPS phase-in and time. The results are similar.

8. Jack Zwanziger, Glenn A. Melnick, and Anil Bamezai, "California Providers Adjust to Increasing Price Competition," in Robert B. Helms, ed., *Health Policy Reform: Competition and Controls* (Washington, D.C.: AEI Press, 1993), pp. 241–58.

selective contracting led to competition that focused on price.[9] The case is only inferential, however.

In more recent work Melnick and colleagues have been able to obtain an index of the transaction prices negotiated by the Blue Cross of California PPO in 1987.[10] The index was the price per day negotiated with each of the 190 hospitals in the statewide PPO network, divided by the average rate per day. They used these data to examine the effects of local hospital competition and bargaining strength on the prices negotiated.

Their regression model controlled for hospital characteristics such as ownership, teaching, relative costliness, and Medicare and Medicaid shares of patient days. Market structure was measured by the Herfindahl Hershman Index; this is the sum of the squared market shares of all hospitals in a hospital's market area. As the number of competitors declines, the index gets larger and the market is more concentrated. Analogously, if there are several hospitals but a single hospital has a very large share of the market, the market is also considered more concentrated and the index value is higher. The bargaining strength of the hospital and of the Blue Cross PPO were measured as the PPO share of the hospital's total days of care and as the hospital's share of the PPO days within its market. The hospital's occupancy rate and the average occupancy rate of all the hospitals in the market were also included in the analysis.

Four findings emerge from this analysis. First, controlling for other factors, the PPO paid a higher price to hospitals located in less competitive markets. Thus, the presence of more local hospitals allowed the PPO to negotiate a lower price. Presumably the PPO

---

9. Jonathan Gruber has argued that Melnick and Zwanziger's findings are the result of an econometric misspecification. If price competition has increased, he argues, hospitals should try to attract patients (and physicians) by increasing quality and amenities *and* cutting price. Thus, hospitals in more competitive markets should have higher costs but lower prices—and smaller profits. In his own data Gruber is able to replicate Melnick and Zwanziger's results. The effects disappear when he includes within-state regional variables. As we discuss below, Gruber does find substantial price reductions, which he attributes to increased hospital competition. See Gruber, "The Effect of Price Shopping," pp. 24–29. It is not obvious, however, that it is appropriate to include the regional variables.

10. Glenn A. Melnick, Jack Zwanziger, Anil Bamezai, and Robert Pattison, "The Effects of Market Structure and Bargaining Position on Hospital Prices," *Journal of Health Economics*, vol. 11, no. 3 (October 1992), pp. 217–33.

was able to raise a credible threat that it would move its patients to another provider.

Second, the larger the percentage of a hospital's total patient days accounted for by the PPO, the greater the leverage the PPO had with the hospital. If the PPO had a larger share of the hospital's business, it was able to negotiate a lower price.[11] Volume of business matters.

Third, the larger the share of the PPO's patients in this market using a hospital, the higher the price the PPO paid. Further, as the number of hospital competitors declined, the PPO paid still more. Thus, the more dependent the PPO was on a hospital, the weaker was the PPO's bargaining position. The difference between points two and three comes down to conflicting loyalties of patients. Patient loyalty to the PPO (and perhaps to its doctors) means that the hospital has to worry that intransigence over price on its part will lead the PPO to channel patients elsewhere. Patient loyalty to the hospital (and perhaps to its doctors) means that, for its part, the PPO must fear that it will lose subscribers if it tries to sever patients' relationships with established providers.

Fourth, high occupancy affects the negotiated price in a straightforward way. Hospitals with high occupancy *located in markets with high average occupancy* charge higher prices to the PPO. Hospitals with high occupancy in other markets do not. Presumably the fear that the PPO will channel its patients to other hospitals in the local market keeps the price down.

This research is important for two reasons. First and most important, it demonstrates that PPOs do compete on a price basis and that the prices actually negotiated are consistent with a rather standard model of firm behavior. Second, the study may suggest why PPOs (and HMOs) negotiate with so many hospitals. A simple view would be that channeling all of one's patients to a single hospital would allow the PPO to negotiate the lowest price. There are dangers associated with this approach, however. As the Melnick team has shown, with this strategy the PPO risks being captured and being charged

---

11. This variable is endogenous, meaning that the price negotiated and the PPO share of the hospital's business are determined simultaneously. This has two implications. First, the coefficient itself is likely to be biased; and second, it may bias the other coefficients in the regression. The authors are able to show that, in spite of this flaw, the other coefficients are stable when the PPO share is excluded from the equation. They are also careful to point out that the variable itself must be interpreted with more than the usual caution.

higher prices by the chosen hospital. It would appear that PPOs are following the example of manufacturing firms and are being careful not to "sole source" their inputs. A simpler explanation is that PPOs must conform to the preferences of their subscribers for greater freedom of choice among hospitals.

Jonathan Gruber has also examined the pricing patterns of hospitals in the California markets.[12] He examined the 1982–1984 and 1984–1988 periods, which encompass the enactment of the PPO legislation and extend the Melnick et al. work by one year. Gruber examined the change in the percentage discount given to all nongovernment payers and the change in the net revenues from nongovernment payers per day. These measures are not unlike the price measures used by Zuckerman in his analysis of cost shifting in the early 1980s.[13] The measure of the hospital's market follows that of Zwanziger and Melnick and is measured by the Herfindahl Index.[14] The regression models controlled for hospital ownership, teaching status, urban-suburban-rural location, and region of the state. In addition, Gruber controlled for the Medicare PPS and included the Medicaid share of patients as a control on the use of selective contracting by the California Medicaid program.

Gruber found that, in the PPO period, hospitals located in more competitive markets had greater increases in the size of the discounts they provided. The average hospital in Los Angeles county, for example, increased its discount by more than 7 percent more than the average hospital in less-competitive northern California. The results based upon average transaction prices also yielded slower price growth in markets with greater hospital competition. Thus, the results are not simply an artifact of hospital strategies to boost list prices in order to grant "discounts" but reflect true price moderation. His analysis of the 1982–1984 period, before the enactment of the pro-PPO legislation, does not show a relationship between hospital competition and hospital discounts. This suggests that the legislation did lead to price competition in the market.

The work by the Melnick team and by Gruber provides strong evidence that hospital pricing in California changed dramatically with the enactment of state laws encouraging selective contracting by private insurers. Gruber reports that by 1989 some twenty-seven states had passed enabling legislation, and in another nineteen the existing insurance regulations could be viewed as not prohibiting the growth

---

12. Jonathan Gruber, "The Effect of Price Shopping."
13. Zuckerman, "Commercial Insurers and All-Payer Regulation."
14. Zwanziger and Melnick, "The Effects of Hospital Competition."

TABLE 6–1
HOSPITAL USE IN AN HMO MARKET AREA

City	HMO	HMO Type	Hospitals in Area	Hospitals Used	Percentage of Hospitals Used
1	A	Staff	71	7	10
	B	IPA	107	46	43
2	C	Staff	36	8	22
3	D	Network	32	15	47
	E	Network	33	8	25
4	F	IPA	53	18	34

SOURCE: Roger Feldman, Hung-Ching Chan, John Kralewski, Bryan Dowd, and Janet Shapiro, "Effects of HMOs on the Creation of Competitive Markets for Hospital Services," *Journal of Health Economics,* vol. 9, no. 3 (September 1990), pp. 211, 212.

of PPOs.[15] If the theory underpinning the California experience is correct, one should see analogous pricing behavior elsewhere in the country. The magnitude of the effects will depend, in part, upon the extent of hospital competition and the freedom of PPOs to contract. The national trends in hospital transaction prices and list prices reported in chapter 3 are consistent with this view.

One non-California study does suggest that insurers are sensitive to the actual prices charged by hospitals and that they channel their patients to preferred hospitals. A team of researchers led by Roger Feldman examined the price sensitivity of six HMOs in four large metropolitan cities in 1986.[16] The four unnamed communities included two immature HMO markets, one of which had only 6 percent of the population enrolled in any of the five operating HMOs. Only one site constituted a well-established HMO market. The six HMOs selected for study had enrollments ranging from 42,000 to 216,000. Two were staff-model HMOs, two were network models, and two were independent practice associations (IPAs).[17] Table 6–1 reports the

15. Gruber, "The Effects of Price Shopping," p. 9.

16. Feldman et al., "Effects of HMOs on the Creation of Competitive Markets."

17. A staff model HMO employs physicians, typically on a salaried basis. A network model tends to contract with only a very limited number of physician group practices. In contrast, an IPA tends to allow all interested physicians to participate.

number of hospitals in each market area and the number of hospitals used by each of the HMOs. Although the IPAs used more hospitals, the staff- and network-model HMOs still admitted patients at 26 percent of the hospitals in their markets, on average.

The Feldman team was interested in two related questions. What effect did price have on the choice of hospitals used, and given the choice of hospitals, what effect did price have on the volume of patients admitted at each hospital? Their analysis of hospital choice used hospital-specific variables including: teaching status, the number of facilities and services reported to the AHA, ownership, central-city location, occupancy, share of beds in the community, and average cost per admission. In addition, they included a set of 1–0 dummies to account for HMO-specific effects.

The Feldman team found that staff- and network-model HMOs were more likely to affiliate with hospitals that had a reputation of high quality. Teaching hospitals and hospitals *not* run by local governments were more likely to be chosen. The model did not do a good job of predicting hospital choice by IPAs. Only higher occupancy had a statistically significant effect. This is not particularly surprising since an IPA, by design, includes a large number of independent physicians who have admitting privileges at a number of different hospitals. It is noteworthy that the average cost per admission had only a small effect and lacked statistical significance for both staff-and-network and IPA-type HMOs. HMOs did not shy away from affiliating with high-cost hospitals. Instead, if anything they choose hospitals with reputations of high quality regardless of cost.

From each HMO the study team obtained the price per admission and the number of admissions at each affiliated hospital. Since price and quantity are simultaneously determined, they estimated a standard two-stage, least-squares regression model. The model was estimated separately for IPA and for staff and network HMOs.

The effects of price on the use of hospitals were quite dramatic (see figure 6–3). A 1 percent increase in the price of an admission led to a 3 percent reduction in the number of admissions for staff- and network-model HMOs. For the IPAs a similar 1 percent increase led to a 1 percent reduction in admissions at the hospital raising its price.

These findings have three implications. First, HMOs are responsive to hospital prices within the set of hospitals with which they affiliate. HMOs apparently will channel patients to hospitals that provide better prices. Second, staff and network HMOs are much more price sensitive, undoubtedly because they are able to contract with a relatively small number of physician groups and to more easily direct patients to preferred hospitals. IPAs have much greater difficulty di-

FIGURE 6–3
EFFECT OF 1 PERCENT INCREASE IN HOSPITAL PRICES ON HMO ADMISSIONS

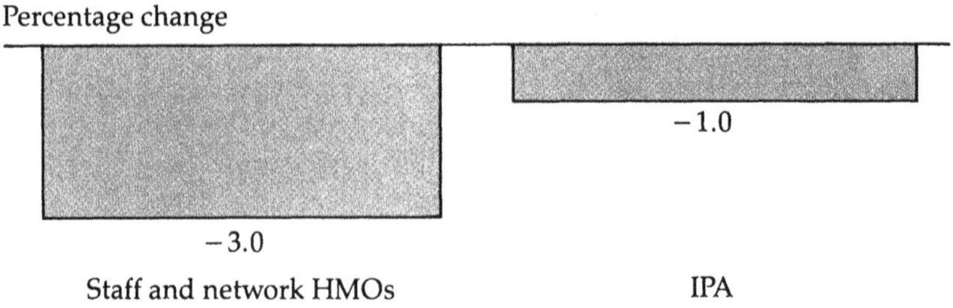

Percentage change

-1.0

-3.0

Staff and network HMOs   IPA

SOURCE: Roger Feldman, Hung-Ching Chan, John Kralewski, Bryan Dowd, and Janet Shapiro, "Effects of HMOs on the Creation of Competitive Markets for Hospital Services," *Journal of Health Economics*, vol. 9, no. 3 (September 1990), p. 220.

recting patients to specific hospitals. Third, this study provides no support for the view that hospitals are able to shift costs to paying HMO patients. Attempts to do so with these payers is a no-win proposition. In the staff and network HMOs an attempt to shift costs would lead to a more-than-proportional reduction in admissions. Rather than earning more revenue from the HMO patients, the hospital loses—and loses big—because of the large reduction in admissions. In the IPA case the reductions in admissions are proportional to increases in price—that is, the hospital does not gain any new revenue; the reductions in volume just offset the gains in price.

There are two broader implications from the Feldman study of six HMOs in four markets. First, price is not the only relevant factor. In their study, the proxy for price (costs per admission) had no effect on the hospitals the HMOs chose to affiliate with. Apparent quality was the determining factor. Price mattered only for the subset of hospitals that met the selection criteria of the HMO.

Second, this study was not undertaken in hotbeds of HMO competition. Given the California experience one would probably not be surprised to see such price sensitivity in markets with substantial PPO or HMO penetration. Rather, only one site was a mature HMO market, and the regression results did not support the view that it dominated the study in any way. Thus even relatively small HMOs (and PPOs) in communities that have only a tradition of conventional insurance coverage appear to be able to channel patients among hospital providers and negotiate hospital prices with the promise of more volume.

70

Summary

One of the key elements in a hospital's ability to shift costs is market power. This chapter examined the effects of market power on hospital pricing behavior. The evidence from the 1970s and early 1980s is consistent. It demonstrates that because health insurance was so widespread consumers had little incentive to seek out lower prices and balance their savings against the quality and service they received. Instead, because high and low quality cost them the same, they had the incentive to seek out high-quality, high-service, high-amenity care. Hospitals then would naturally compete for patients (and their physician agents) on the basis of quality, service, and amenities. The empirical analysis from this period supports the view that hospitals in more competitive communities offered more services and had higher costs as a result.

The evidence of the past ten years is startlingly different from that which preceded it. This evidence is not clearly generalizable, coming as it does largely from the California experience. Nonetheless, the evidence suggests that preferred provider organizations have been able to negotiate hospital transaction prices that are well below list prices. More important, these prices appear to behave as traditional economic theory would suggest. When hospital markets are less concentrated, PPOs are able to get lower prices.

The evidence is not confined entirely to California. Evidence from four metropolitan areas with greatly differing degrees of HMO penetration indicates that HMOs have been successful in negotiating prices and enforcing price concessions by making credible threats to channel patients elsewhere. This evidence is somewhat inferential. Strictly, what it says is that the HMOs in the study admitted substantially more patients to hospitals from which they had received a lower price. For staff and network HMOs a 10 percent increase in price was associated with a 30 percent reduction in admissions. This work also suggested that price is not the only relevant factor. HMOs first affiliated with hospitals that had what might be called "badges of quality:" teaching programs and nongovernment ownership. Indeed, there was no evidence that HMOs chose to be affiliated with hospitals on the basis of price, only that price mattered once the hospital had passed the quality test.

This work suggests that the growth in price competition over the past decade has severely limited the magnitude of any dynamic cost shifting that may have been going on. Certainly areas of the country exist where there is only limited hospital price competition. In these areas cost shifting, given the other necessary conditions, could be

71

continuing. But given the widening gap between national trends in list and transaction prices reported in chapter 3 and the evidence of a mechanism to accomplish price reductions documented here, one must at least entertain the conclusion that dynamic cost shifting is not an important phenomenon in much of the hospital industry today.

7
Employer Cost Shifting

Thus far we have focused on cost shifting in the health care setting. We considered price discrimination or static cost shifting and concluded that providers do charge different prices to different payers. We also considered the much more important issue of dynamic cost shifting in which a provider raises the price to one payer *because* he has been compelled to lower the price to some other payer. We found limited, but very old, evidence of this and recent evidence which suggests that the ability to cost shift has eroded dramatically even if the desire to do so has not.

In this chapter we turn our attention to employers and cost shifting. Cost shifting by providers is said to increase the costs of health care to employers. The usual argument is that hospitals and others provide care to the uninsured; health care providers pay for this care by charging higher prices to insurers, which in turn charge higher premiums to employers. The costs are thus "shifted" to employers. The policy prescription is usually to establish a government program that provides care for the uninsured. The theory is that employers insurance premiums will fall in response.

"Cost shifting" is also used to describe what happens when (typically) small employers do not provide health insurance to their employees. The (typically) large employer does. The costs of health insurance are "shifted" from the small employer to the large because the large employer provides health insurance for its employees as well as coverage for its employees' dependents. The policy prescription is usually to require the small employer to provide coverage, thereby paying his "share" of the costs and lowering the costs to the large employer. The size of firms (large and small) is not important to the argument, only the fact that some firms offer insurance and some do not.

In this chapter we examine the nature of employers' labor costs, why employers offer insurance, and how the insurance is paid for. We also examine the empirical evidence which suggests that workers, not their employers, pay for health insurance. We then examine the effects of cost shifting on employers and workers, and we look at the consequences for workers and their employers of public policy proposals to deal with cost shifting.

The Nature of Labor Markets

In principle, labor markets are quite simple. Firms hire workers as long as the value of the goods and services they produce is greater than or equal to the wages they are paid. If the firm pays too little, it will have trouble attracting and keeping workers and will forgo profits. If it pays too much, it will have no trouble getting and keeping workers but will be spending profits the owners could have used for other purposes.

The labor market is much more complex than this, of course. Workers come with different productive capabilities. Jobs come with different characteristics; some are dangerous, dirty, and disagreeable. Some are not. Most are somewhere in between. One of the features of the labor market is its ability to account for these different capabilities and characteristics. There is good empirical evidence, for example, that more experienced and more highly educated workers receive higher compensation. There is also reliable evidence that, controlling for other factors, riskier jobs and jobs in less desirable locations pay better.[1] The more experienced workers produce more and justify the higher pay. The risky jobs in forlorn locations yield higher pay because it is cheaper for the employer to pay higher levels of compensation than to reduce the risk or to move the firm.

The form in which compensation is paid can also vary. Some firms offer money wages and health insurance. Others offer money wages, health insurance, and parking. Some offer only money wages. The question is why. The answer is that the form of the compensation bundle depends on both worker preferences and the costs to the employer.

Worker preferences are crucial; if workers do not value a particular form of payment, it does not count as payment. A firm located in downtown Washington, D.C., for example, may seek to attract office clerks by providing them parking places. Given the excellent subway system in the city, this form of compensation is not likely to be highly valued (unless workers can lease their spots). In any event, its value to the employee is unlikely to be valued as high as the cost to the employer of providing it.

The cost of providing each type of compensation is the other key

---

1. Ronald G. Ehrenberg and Robert S. Smith, *Modern Labor Economics*, 2nd ed. (Glenview, Ill.: Scott, Foresman and Co., 1985), pp. 219–52.

element in determining the form of employee compensation. A dollar of take-home pay costs the employer a dollar plus the applicable federal, state, and city taxes. A parking space costs what it would fetch in the open market. A health insurance plan costs the premium the employer would have to pay.

It comes as no surprise, then, that the compensation bundle used by an employer is that which yields the smallest total labor bill consistent with employee preferences. This simple rule has important implications for the complex world of employer-sponsored health insurance.

First, it implies that firms will offer health insurance only if their workers value it sufficiently. Surveys of workers commonly find that health insurance is the most highly valued benefit. Not everyone has this preference, however. Some view themselves as so unlikely to be stricken by illness or injury that health insurance, though valuable, is not as valuable as some other things. People in the United States between the ages of fifteen and forty-four had only a 6 percent chance of being hospitalized in 1990. Those aged forty-five to sixty-four were more than twice as likely to be hospitalized.[2] The younger cohort finds hospitalization insurance less valuable. They might seek out firms that offer less health insurance, or no health insurance, and more of other, more valuable, forms of compensation.

In addition, some workers have health insurance provided by the employer of their parent or spouse (we will deal with the cost shifting elements of this shortly), so health insurance offered by their own employers is of little value. To them, any value of employer-provided health insurance lies in the dual coverage they receive, which reduces out-of-pocket payments, covers additional services, or provides protection if a spouse or parent loses coverage. But many of these individuals would trade this additional coverage or security for other, more highly valued forms of compensation—such as cash. They might seek out firms that gave them a more valuable compensation bundle.

Second, a firm will offer health insurance only if it is less costly than other forms of payment. There are three general reasons why a firm may find it less costly to offer insurance: tax laws, administrative cost savings, and "favorable selection." Health insurance is a deductible business expense, and it is exempt from federal and state personal income taxes and social security taxes. Thus, as long as workers value health insurance sufficiently, to an employer a dollar of health

---

2. Department of Health and Human Services, *Health United States 1991* (Washington, D.C.: Public Health Service, May 1992), p. 224.

insurance is cheaper than a dollar plus taxes of money wages.

There may be administrative cost savings as well. Group insurance is less expensive to sell than individually purchased coverage. This difference will be reflected in premiums in a reasonably competitive insurance market. In addition, there may be economies of scope in the firm's personnel office. Because it keeps records for personnel reasons, new records need not be created for health insurance reasons.

Perhaps the most important reason why employers may have lower costs if they offer health insurance, however, is favorable selection. Employed persons are likely to be lower utilizers of health services than would a simple random sample of the population, even one matched by age, sex, and gender. And they are certainly lower utilizers of health services than any matched cohort that is not employed. In fact, some of the unemployed are unemployed for health reasons. The fact that the employed cohort is healthy enough to hold down a job serves as an effective (and cheap) device to separate lower utilizers from higher utilizers. This is "favorable selection." In a reasonably competitive insurance market this lower expected claims experience is reflected in a smaller premium.[3] Thus, if the firm can purchase health insurance more cheaply than a worker can on her own, and she values that coverage, the firm will find it profitable to provide it.

The third implication of the simple model of employer-sponsored health insurance is that those workers who value health insurance the least will disproportionately end up working for firms that have the highest cost of providing health insurance.[4] The explanation is simple. Workers who do not value health insurance highly will be more attracted to firms that provide higher money wages than to those that provide lower money wages and more insurance. Analogously, firms that find health insurance more costly will try to structure compensation bundles that are light on health insurance and heavy on other elements.

---

3. Don't make too much of the competitive requirement. Self-insured firms will not generally find it profitable to charge monopoly prices to themselves. Indeed, one explanation for the growth in self-insured firms was the attempt by employers to avoid insurance premiums that were set above costs. Other explanations include avoidance of mandated benefits, premium taxes, and high-risk pools.

4. See Gerald S. Goldstein and Mark V. Pauly, "Group Health Insurance as a Local Public Good," in Richard N. Rosett, ed., *The Role of Health Insurance in the Health Services Sector*, pp. 73–109 (New York: National Bureau of Economic Research, 1976).

Some firms find health insurance more costly because they are too small to take advantage of any administrative cost savings. They may produce a seasonal product or otherwise employ a work force that turns over frequently. High employee turnover raises the administrative costs of providing coverage.[5] Finally, some firms may not obtain favorable selection. Deborah Chollet argues that small firms may actually be subject to adverse selection.[6] A firm may put Uncle Ned on the payroll so that his prostate surgery will be covered, for example. This is not to say that all or most small firms engage in such behavior; however, if it is a relatively common practice and if insurers have no cost-effective mechanism for identifying the firms that do it, then premiums to small firms will reflect the higher claims experience.

The fourth implication of the model of labor compensation is the most important for our purposes. It says that workers pay for health insurance largely in the form of money wages and other benefits given up. This means that, controlling for other things, firms that offer health insurance pay lower wages.

Theory says that firms will pay as little as possible to get the output they desire. They will try to find the combination of wages, health insurance, parking, and other benefits that gets the desired amount of labor at the lowest cost. If the firm can buy health insurance more cheaply than the worker can individually, and the worker values health insurance highly, the firm is happy to provide health insurance. That insurance, however, is paid for through lower wages, less parking, or reductions in other benefits.

This view of labor compensation is of critical importance to our understanding of employer cost shifting and the effects of provider cost. It says that small firms without health insurance do not shift costs to large firms that offer insurance. Rather, wages adjust in both firms and nothing is shifted. Those who argue that cost shifting occurs say that the funds flow from the insurance plan of the large firm to the medical provider of the dependent employed by the smaller

---

5. High administrative costs alone are not a sufficient reason for employers not to offer health coverage. If workers valued insurance coverage sufficiently, the market would see that they got it. One reason many construction workers get coverage through their union or work hall is that they change employers often. The union coverage reduces the transaction costs associated with turnover. Similarly, part-time status is not an explanation, in and of itself, for lack of coverage.

6. Deborah Chollet, "Uninsured Workers: Sources and Dimensions of the Problem," paper presented at the Allied Social Sciences Association meeting, New York, December 28, 1988.

firm, but they have neglected to account for the lower wages paid by the large firm and the higher wages paid by the smaller firm.

Evidence of Compensating Wage Adjustment

A growing body of empirical research supports the argument that compensating wage and benefit adjustments are made in the labor market. Although no studies have directly examined the allegation that employers cost shift, the evidence on health insurance, workers' compensation, and pensions does support the view that compensating differentials exist. All of these imply that the employer cost shifting story is incorrect.

The empirical problem is a difficult one; although the theory is simple, the employment world is complex. If we want to determine whether money wages are lower in firms that offer health insurance, we must compare similar circumstances. We will want to control for differences in working conditions and the presence and magnitude of other fringe benefits. We will also want to control for differences in worker characteristics. Consider a firm that pays wages and benefits that are higher than a competitor's. The firm will have its choice of workers, and one would expect it to hire those who seem better motivated, more dependable, more competitive, and more aggressive. If the researcher is unable to effectively control for these differences, he is likely to observe a positive relationship between fringe benefits and wages. The estimated effect of benefits is biased, however. It is picking up the effect of both the greater productivity of the workers in this firm and the tradeoff between benefits and wages. The early literature was fraught with these problems.[7]

In the strongest health insurance evidence to date, Jonathan Gruber used Current Population Survey data from 1974–1975 and 1977–1978 to examine the effects of state laws mandating the inclusion of maternity benefits in employer-sponsored health insurance.[8] If wages adjust in response to such mandates, we would expect to see lower wages for workers in states where employers are required to provide maternity benefits. If wages could be fine tuned, we would expect different cohorts of workers to be affected differently. Male

---

7. For a discussion, see Michael A. Morrisey, "Mandated Benefits and Compensating Differentials—Taxing the Uninsured," in Robert Helms, ed., *American Health Policy: Critical Issues for Reform*, pp. 133–51 (Washington, D.C.: AEI Press, 1993).

8. Jonathan Gruber, "The Effect of a Group-Specific Mandated Benefit: Evidence from Health Insurance Benefits for Maternity," National Bureau of Economic Research, working paper 4157 (Cambridge, Mass., 1992).

and female workers over, say, age forty would be virtually unaffected. Single men would be unaffected. Employed married women of child-bearing ages, say ages twenty to forty, would be most at risk of seeing their wages reduced to pay for the new benefit, although single women and men married to women in this age group would also be affected.

Gruber ran wage regressions for workers in three states that enacted the mandate (Illinois, New Jersey, and New York) and five states that did not (Ohio, Indiana, North Carolina, Connecticut, and Massachusetts). He controlled for education, experience, gender, marital status, race, union status, and industry in which the worker was employed. In addition, he included 1–0 variables to account for whether the worker was in a state that enacted the mandate, whether the worker was a member of the "treatment group" (twenty- to forty-year-old married females), and interactions between mandates and treatment group. He hypothesized that if wages adjust, he would find that twenty- to forty-year-old married females in states that adopted the mandate would have lower wages than similar women both before the mandate and in states that did not adopt the mandate, controlling for education, experience, and the other factors noted above.

This is precisely what Gruber found. The inflation-adjusted wages of "at-risk" women in the states that mandated maternity benefits declined by 4.3 percent. Using actuarial estimates of the cost of maternity coverage, it can be determined that the full costs of the maternity benefit were paid by this cohort.

Gruber also calculated the effect of the federal Pregnancy Discrimination Act of 1978. This law required all health insurance plans to treat pregnancy the same way it would treat an illness. Here controlling for other factors is more difficult. Nonetheless, Gruber found that 63–90 percent of the cost of the coverage was paid by the affected workers. This is strong evidence that workers pay for health insurance benefits in the form of lower wages.

Stephen Woodbury and Wei-Jang Huang have also examined the nature of substitute forms of compensation.[9] They examined 1969–1982 data drawn from the industry reports used to compile the National Income and Product Accounts and the 1977 Survey of Employer Expenditures for Employee Compensation conducted by the Bureau of Labor Statistics. They ran a series of regressions that esti-

---

9. Stephen A. Woodbury and Wei-Jang Huang, *The Tax Treatment of Fringe Benefits* (Kalamazoo, Mich.: W. E. Upjohn Institute for Employment Research, 1991).

mated substitution elasticities for different forms of payment. The easiest way to interpret their results is to examine the effects of various policy simulations. The 1986 Tax Reform Act (the so-called Reagan tax cuts) reduced the marginal tax rate on money income but did not affect the tax status of pensions and health insurance. Woodbury and Huang estimate that this change led to an average increase in wage expenditures of 1.6 percent, a reduction in health insurance expenditures of 6.1 percent, and a reduction in pension contributions of 18.5 percent.[10] If health insurance benefits were taxed at the same rate as money income, Woodbury and Huang estimate that the substitution effect would lead to a nearly 17 percent reduction in expenditures on health insurance, a 1.6 percent increase in pensions (as workers substitute untaxed pension contributions for taxed health insurance), and a .7 percent increase in money wages.

Research on workers' compensation and pension benefits suffers from many of the same methodological problems that health insurance does, and the more recent efforts in these fields have also found ways to overcome them.

In the best of the workers' compensation research, Kip Viscusi and Michael Moore used detailed data on state workers' compensation programs.[11] They were able to link the amount of benefits to the actual risk of work-place injury. This is important because using average risk rates tends to bias the workers' compensation–wage tradeoff toward zero. Using 1977 IRS data, Viscusi and Moore found that a one-dollar increase in the workers' compensation benefit resulted in a wage reduction of twelve cents per hour. The finding was statistically significant. Since the actuarially fair cost of the workers' compensation coverage was five cents an hour, the wage reduction more than fully compensates for the cost of the insurance.[12]

Using different data sets from 1977 and 1983, Moore and Viscusi again found wage reductions that more than fully offset the cost of workers' compensation insurance.[13] Jonathan Gruber and Alan

---

10. It is important to note that the tax laws also generated income as well as substitution effects. The income effects led to increased demand for all forms of compensation. Ibid., pp. 154–55.

11. W. Kip Viscusi and Michael J. Moore, "Workers' Compensation: Wage Effects, Benefit Inadequacies, and the Value of Health Losses," *Review of Economics and Statistics*, vol. 69, no. 2 (May 1987), pp. 243–63.

12. Since one expects workers to be risk averse, this overadjustment is not unexpected. Risk aversion means that workers are willing to pay more than the expected loss to avoid the consequences of a loss. Risk aversion is, ultimately, the reason why insurance of any form exists.

13. Michael J. Moore and W. Kip Viscusi, *Compensation Mechanisms for Job Risks* (Princeton, N.J.: Princeton University Press, 1990).

Krueger used Current Population Survey data from the early and late 1980s to examine wages and workers' compensation benefits for privately employed carpenters, truck drivers, nonprofessional hospital employees, gasoline station employees, and plumbers.[14] Although the results vary by occupation, when combined they indicated that more than 86 percent of the cost of workers' compensation insurance was borne by workers in the form of reduced wages.

In addition to the problems of measurement and adjustment for worker productivity noted above, the analysis of pensions is further complicated by the compensating wage differential, which requires workers to give up wages today for the promise of pension benefits ten or twenty years from now. The early literature tried to find evidence of such a tradeoff but was unsuccessful.[15]

To my knowledge, Edward Montgomery and colleagues have offered the only empirical test of the lifetime model of pensions.[16] They matched 1983 Survey of Consumer Finances data (from the IRS) with detailed information on pension plans and demographic characteristics of individual workers. Using the wage today–pension tomorrow model they find only negligible evidence of a tradeoff between wages and pensions. But when lifetime wages were imputed and used in the models, they found a coefficient of $-.8$, suggesting that 80 percent of the pension was paid for by lifetime wages. Since workers do frequently die before retirement, pension plans do fail on occasion, and workers are often terminated before retirement, the 80 percent adjustment appears to be reasonable. Indeed, it is dramatic evidence that wages adjust to other benefits in the compensation bundle.

Implications for Employer Cost Shifting

The empirical literature supports the proposition that wages (and/or other benefits) are lower in the presence of health insurance. This has

14. Jonathan Gruber and Alan B. Krueger, "The Incidence of Mandated Employer-Provided Insurance: Lessons from Workers' Compensation Insurance," working paper 3557, New York: National Bureau of Economic Research, 1990. It is worth noting that if the Viscusi and Moore model is correct, the Gruber and Krueger model may be misspecified and the estimate of the wage effect may be understated in their work.

15. For excellent discussions of the problems and the early literature, see Charles Brown, "Comment," in Jack E. Triplett, ed., *The Measurement of Labor Cost* (Chicago: University of Chicago Press, 1983), pp. 367–68; and Richard A. Ippolito, "The Implicit Pension Contract: Developments and New Directions," *Journal of Human Resources*, vol. 22, no. 4 (1987), pp. 441–67.

16. Edward Montgomery, Kathryn Shaw, and Mary Ellen Benedict, "Pensions and Wages: An Hedonic Price Theory Approach," National Bureau of Economic Research, working paper 3458 (New York, 1990).

important implications for how we view cost shifting in its several forms.

First, consider the allegation that small uninsured firms shift health care costs to the large firms that provide coverage to dependents and spouses. The evidence on compensating differentials says this does not happen, or at least it does not happen once wages have had a chance to adjust. Suppose an employer mandate is enacted requiring the small firm to provide health insurance to its workers. The inference from the case that cost-shifting takes place is that large firms will see their health insurance costs decline and small employers will themselves be faced with insurance premiums. In fact, this will be true initially, but wages will adjust and the savings to the typical large firm will be short-lived. The health insurance package becomes less valuable. Workers in the large firm will want to be paid what they are still worth, and wages or other benefits will have to increase to maintain a stable labor force.[17] Although the small firm does face health insurance premiums for the first time, it is able to reduce wages.

Does this mean that there are no effects on employers? Not entirely. Remember that workers and firms sorted themselves on the basis of preferences and the costs of wages and benefits. Now workers (in the typically small firms) who valued benefits less than the money wages must trade money wages for health benefits.[18] But they do not value the benefits as highly and will not accept a dollar-for-dollar tradeoff. Some will only work if the compensation bundle is worth *to them* at least what it was before. In other words, the employer's labor compensation bill will be somewhat higher, and consequently employment will be somewhat lower. The extent of unemployment will depend upon how much or how little the currently uninsured workers value the health insurance. If it is little valued, the unemployment effects will be larger.

The major unemployment effects of a mandated health insurance program occur when wages are at or near the minimum wage. In this

---

17. Our discussion assumes a labor market in equilibrium. If demand has declined in an industry and it is seeking to reduce its work force, total labor compensation will certainly decline. In such a market wages will not increase enough to offset the decline in health insurance, but the reduction in compensation is not the result of the mandate. Rather, it results from the decline in the demand for labor.

18. Large firms are also affected. Health insurance was less costly to them. They must substitute more expensive money wages (and other benefits) for dependent health insurance. The higher labor costs here also lead to some reductions in employment.

instance wages cannot legally adjust downward. As a consequence, some jobs no longer produce a product worth the minimum wage plus health benefits.

The other issue is provider cost shifting and its effects on employers. We have already addressed this issue. Suppose a hospital wishes to provide care to the uninsured. It would do so by spending some of its profit or surplus for this purpose. This has no effect on the employer under most cost-shifting models. If the hospital is maximizing profits for stockholders or maximizing surplus to provide care to the indigent, hospital prices will be exactly the same and will reflect the extent of price sensitivity in the hospital market. If the hospital did not spend its surplus on the indigent, one would expect it to spend it on something else. Thus, hospitals have not shifted the costs of the uninsured to employers. Rather, they have charged employers what the traffic will bear. Employers would, therefore, be better advised to worry less about cost shifting, and worry more about enhancing price competition and finding hospitals that charge lower prices for equivalent care.

The final issue is provider cost shifting. We argued in earlier chapters that static cost shifting or price discrimination has been a characteristic of health care markets for a long time. (This activity is distinct from dynamic cost shifting, which appears to be increasingly a nonissue and may *never* have been an issue.) Suppose the government were effectively to encourage increased price competition. The resultant price reductions would imply lower insurance premiums, which would reduce labor costs. Firms would then seek to hire more workers, and labor compensation would be bid up.

Summary

The theory and the recent empirical evidence on labor compensation suggest that workers pay for the health insurance they receive largely in the form of lower money wages and reduced benefits. The implication is that firms that do not provide health insurance do not shift costs to insured firms. Although the insured firm pays higher medical claims and higher insurance premiums to cover employees' spouses and dependents, it also pays lower money wages. Firms without health insurance must pay higher wages to attract equally skilled workers.

8
Conclusions and Implications

This monograph has examined the issue of cost shifting from a variety of perspectives. It has examined the theoretical underpinnings and has reviewed the empirical literature. What do we know? The theory led to four conclusions:

- To successfully charge different prices to different payers—that is, to engage in static cost shifting—a medical care provider must have market power. In the absence of market power, payers faced with the higher prices will obtain care elsewhere.
- Providers that are concerned only about profits will not engage in dynamic cost shifting. That is, they will not find it profitable to raise the price to one category of payers in response to a price cut from another payer. Since this sort of provider will set prices to get the most profit possible from each payer category, raising the price to one group necessarily reduces the profit obtained from that group.
- Providers that value other things in addition to profits will not necessarily engage in dynamic cost shifting. A provider that values profits and care for the poor, for example, will not raise its prices to paying patients when it has more poor to care for. This provider serves the poor by extracting all the profits possible from paying patients and spending some, or all, on the poor. If the provider raises the prices to paying patients, even for this noble cause, it finds that profits are reduced. *The only difference between the profit-maximizing provider and the one caring for the poor is in how they spend their profits.*
- For dynamic cost shifting to exist a provider must have *unexploited* market power. It "favors" paying patients and so has not been charging them as much as profit maximization would allow. If Medicare reduced its payments to this provider, for example, the provider would raise prices to the private payers it serves. It can only do this, however, until private payers are paying the profit-maximizing price. Once this happens, further attempts at dynamic cost shifting lead to smaller profits from the paying patients.

The rigorous empirical literature yields three findings:

- Hospitals (and other providers) do charge different prices to different payers.

• These differences do not appear to be justified on the basis of differences in the average cost of providing care. Thus, price discrimination, or static cost shifting, does exist and indeed is common in the hospital industry.

• There is no evidence that hospitals have been able to completely offset price reductions to one group by raising prices to others.

The evidence on dynamic cost shifting consists of four studies, three conducted before the advent of the Medicare PPS and the growth of managed care. The evidence supporting the existence of cost shifting found that prices charged to privately insured patients increased by 50 percent (1981–1983 data) and 90 percent (1979 data) in response to cuts in government programs and discounts to other payers. Thus, dynamic cost shifting, even in the strongest supporting evidence, does not succeed completely.

The evidence disputing the notion that cost shifting is prevalent found that as a hospital's reliance on commercial insurers grew, the extent to which it raised prices to these payers in the face of government cuts or increases in charity care declined. Indeed, when a hospital's reliance on commercial insurance reached the hospital average, 25 percent, its prices to commercial insurers actually declined even as its "need to cost shift" increased. This study, however, was based on 1981–1983 data. Other evidence comes from a mid-1980s study of Blue Cross data. It found that Blue Cross *saved* money after the Medicare PPS was implemented.

There is more current, albeit indirect, evidence that cost shifting has not been a financial panacea for hospitals. First, reductions in Medicaid payment levels have caused some hospitals to cut back or eliminate their care for Medicaid patients. Studies of California hospitals find that hospitals have lowered their prices in response to the growth of managed care. These price cuts are deeper where hospitals face more competition, and the amount of charity care provided falls in the face of these price cuts. None of these responses supports the idea that cost shifting works.

What Is One to Make of All This?

In my judgment, hospitals today generally have little ability to engage in dynamic cost shifting. Instead, hospitals are best viewed as following the rule of thumb that says "no margin, no mission." They charge high prices to patients who will pay them and lower prices to others. Hospitals charge all they can to insured patients and use the proceeds for a variety of good things, including care for the indigent. Thus,

one should think of hospitals as charging high prices to some patients, who generate profits, which in turn are spent on care for the
uninsured. The logic runs from prices to the uninsured, not the other
way around. The presence of more uninsured does not lead to higher
prices; rather, higher prices have allowed hospitals to care for the uninsured.

These results have enormous policy implications. Suppose the
number of indigents were to suddenly drop to zero. Those who say
that hospitals cost shift would say that prices to private payers would
fall. I do not believe that would happen. Instead, if the indigent were
to suddenly disappear, hospitals would spend their surpluses on
other good things: more technology, more research, nicer waiting
rooms and physician suites, and thicker carpets in administration.
Only if a hospital "likes" paying patients should we expect it to drop
its prices. This seems like an awfully thin reed on which to hang so
much public policy.

Implications for Policy

We began by discussing a number of public statements about cost
shifting and some common perceptions of how the health care sector
responds to policy changes. Let us return to that topic and discuss
how it is more likely to respond.

1. *Medicare errs in determining payments, or Medicare or Medicaid reduce
payment levels.*

First, hospitals will have lower profits; as a result they will have
less to spend on charity care, new equipment, etc. Second, significant
reductions in payments from Medicare and Medicaid will result in
reduced services to their beneficiaries. Although we have not seen
hospitals drop out of the Medicare market, we have seen reductions
in lengths of stay and admission rates for Medicare beneficiaries. We
have seen hospitals cut back on the number of Medicaid patients they
admit and cease to admit Medicaid patients altogether.

2. *HMOs, PPOs, or other private insurers negotiate price cuts.*

Rather than leading to higher prices to other private patients,
there is evidence that these cuts reduce hospital profits. The evidence
also indicates that the level of charity care provided by these hospitals
is reduced. These changes are inconsistent with the argument that
hospitals have the power to make up for losses by raising prices to
others. In fact, many hospital representatives assert that there is no
one to cost shift to. When hospitals raise prices to other private insurers, those insurers raise premiums and find that people drop cover-

age. This is an admission that dynamic cost shifting is an unsuccessful strategy.

In all of this one must be careful to look behind hospital sticker prices. The relevant price is not the hospital's list price. What matters is the actual price paid. There is growing evidence that the spread between list and transaction prices has grown over the past several years. While the sticker price has risen rapidly, the actual price has gone up much more slowly.

3. *The government insures the uninsured.*

The Clinton administration and others have argued that providing health insurance for the uninsured will result in lower prices to the currently insured because hospitals will no longer have to charge such high prices. My analysis of the hospital market does not support this view. Providing such coverage is a laudable objective. But suggesting that this action, in and of itself, will lower prices is overreaching.

Instead, the new coverage will mean that hospitals no longer have to spend hospital profits on the uninsured. They will be able to spend their profits on other things. Hospitals will not reduce prices to privately insured patients unless, as we noted above, hospitals "favor" paying patients.

The implications of expanding insurance coverage to the uninsured are actually even more depressing. Because heretofore uninsured patients will be able to pay for their care, they will in effect be bidding with currently insured patients for the available hospital capacity. The economic model says that the *transaction prices paid by currently insured patients will actually increase.*

The Clinton administration proposal and the host of other proposals on the street may include very effective means of controlling health care costs, but providing coverage to the uninsured, in and of itself, is not one of them. Expanded coverage is not a cost-containment device.

4. *All payers do not pay their fair share of costs.*

Providers and some insurers have argued that it is unfair for the government and some private insurers to pay lower prices than others. They argue that those paying the higher prices have been subsidizing those paying the lower prices. Two related responses to this claim make the case that cost shifting does not work. There is in fact no evidence that one group subsidizes another. There is, however, a serious question about how hospitals cover their fixed costs in the long run.

First, providers do charge different prices to different payers.

One group of payers lacks market clout and pays more. The solution is to find ways to eliminate the market power enjoyed by the hospital or to obtain more market power as a buyer. It may seem unfair to some, but it is how competitive markets work things out.

The second response relies on the cost theory discussed in chapter 4. It may be that hospital patients of all payer categories have equal average costs. It may even be true that Medicare patients have higher average costs. The marginal costs of treating additional patients may, however, actually be less than average costs. If so, the prices paid by Medicare, Medicaid, or managed-care plans may cover the marginal operating costs associated with their care and perhaps make a contribution to fixed costs. Costs are no more shifted in this case than in the case of the airline that sells some seats at prices below average cost.

The issue is that marginal costs are less than average costs. In the long run both the fixed costs and the operating costs must be covered. There are several ways of doing this. One is to charge higher prices to those who are willing and able to pay and to set prices at marginal cost for the rest. Arguably this is what hospitals have been doing. This is a stable long-run solution as long as the group paying the higher prices is willing and able to pay.

The growth of PPOs and managed-care plans that negotiate with hospitals on the basis of price, however, suggest that this may not be a stable real-world solution. Just as in the airlines, we should expect prices for all classes of patients to fall to marginal cost as providers compete. As the short run becomes the long run, capital must be replaced, but sufficient funds will be unavailable to do so. Some hospitals will close; others will have more patients. Marginal costs and prices will rise at these hospitals. Ultimately, all remaining hospitals will cover their costs by charging prices higher than those charged during the intervening years before the excess capacity was squeezed out. This may be a painful process for some, but it is the most efficient way we know to adjust an industry's capacity to changing market conditions.

5. *Employers must provide health insurance.*

The prior argument explains why increased coverage for the uninsured will not reduce hospital prices. Thus, employers that are currently providing health insurance will not save money as a result of an expansion of coverage.

What about requiring all firms to provide health insurance to their workers? Labor market theory and evidence suggest that this requirement is unlikely to have much effect on firms currently providing insurance. Employed spouses and dependents would receive insurance through their own employers. Individual firms could therefore expect to pay less in medical claims and lower insurance premiums. These firms should expect wages to adjust upward, however, because current workers would initially be getting a compensation package that is worth less while they are providing the same output.

Analogously, firms that do not currently provide health insurance would have to do so; they should expect to be able to cut wages or to raise them more slowly to compensate for the cost of the health insurance premiums. To the extent that wages cannot adjust, however, unemployment will result.

What Is to Be Done?

It is abundantly clear that providers do charge different prices to different payers. I do not believe that providing health insurance to the uninsured will change this fact. Indeed, it is very likely that providing insurance to the currently uninsured will increase the prices paid by the currently insured. This is not to say society should not find a way to provide insurance for those who cannot afford it. The price problem, however, must be approached directly.

It is not the purpose of this book to discuss the relative merits of various approaches to achieving cost containment. The presence of different prices for the same service is, however, evidence of market power on the part of hospitals. A market-based approach would find ways to encourage price competition on the part of hospitals and other providers. As we saw in chapter 6, there is evidence from California and from HMOs elsewhere that insurers can negotiate lower prices and that insurers are able to channel patients to those affiliated hospitals. There have been dramatic changes in these markets as a result of the encouragement of price competition. Given nearly thirty years of payment systems that have not encouraged price shopping in health care, the measures of success we have seen, together with the fear and trembling observed in other regional health care markets, suggests that a much greater reliance on price competition in health care may yield substantial benefits.

A NOTE ON THE BOOK

This book was edited by
Cheryl Weissman
of the AEI Press.
The text was set in Palatino, a typeface designed by
the twentieth-century Swiss designer Hermann Zapf.
Coghill Composition, of Richmond, Virginia,
set the type, and Data Reproductions Corporation,
of Rochester Hills, Michigan, printed and bound the book,
using permanent acid-free paper.

The AEI PRESS is the publisher for the American Enterprise Institute for Public Policy Research, 1150 17th Street, N.W., Washington, D.C. 20036; *Christopher C. DeMuth*, publisher; *Dana Lane*, director; *Ann Petty*, editor; *Cheryl Weissman*, editor; *Lisa Roman*, editorial assistant (rights and permissions).